The Perfect Rose

By

Loretta V

1stBooks – rev. 12/28/01

Dedications

First of all I would like to give thanks to my Lord and savior Jesus Christ, for inspiring me to write these words. Next of all to my family, whom I love very much, I thank God for having them in my life. And to my dear friend in Christ Everett Rucker, for his financial and spiritual support in being so persistence in leading me to send my writings out so others might get a closer walk with God. And last but not least I would like to give thanks to my sister in Christ Nicki Tilford, who did a excellent job in editing my book.

Table of Contents

Introduction

As you read these mighty teachings, you will experience a variety of feelings. This writer has surrendered to allow herself to be used as a vessel by God to express in a plain-spoken manner about her life's experiences. Her choice was to share these writings with hundreds of people each time she completed one. She mailed them to individuals as she was guided with no thought except to inspire, encourage and expose much of life's hurt and pain. In the midst of this practice, one of the recipients felt her "reach" should be expanded and offered support to create this book. It was the hand of God at work. Loretta was stunned — but she gathered herself together to prepare for this new level.

She continues to allow her words to be "moved out" by God onto the pages. We believe that many will be touched by the messages and may experience clarification or revelation. God moves in mysterious ways His wonders to perform. He also calls the emotionally hurting, abandoned and abused to allow Him to use their stories to remind us of matters too many have forgotten, avoided, denied or ignored. Pain and suffering ravage this earth in ways and forms never intended. Sister Loretta V. reveals much that we might consider, ponder and lift in prayer.

Surely her heart is a blessing and how deeply she cares is evident. We certainly need more people like her. Though she obviously has had her share of heartache, she has been blessed with a sustaining abundance called love. Loretta's desire is for us to truly learn to love the way God intended so that we can sincerely love one another. She has traveled a road that would certainly have caused another to falter or fatigue. But she draws her strength from an unrelenting faith in God through Jesus Christ, her Lord and Savior.

A Personal Prayer

I know that you are a Prince of Peace. I want you to be my Savior and Father. I want to know you personally. We say all of the time, "Lord, I want you to control my heart". Do we really mean that? I want you to control my life and mind and soul. We worry so much about what others think about us so we try to put on "airs" so we will be noticed. We spend so much time trying to talk proper, holding back all of the slang that we use — trying to impress others. But Father, help me not to worry about what others think of me. Help me to have a closer walk with thee because I can't impress you Father by putting on a false front. I have to be true with you. You know my heart. You are completely aware of my shortcomings. I could never hide anything from you. Teach me Father to be humble. I want a relationship with you like Adam and Eve had before sin entered in. I want to really learn how to pray to you Father. I want to learn how to talk to you. I want to know how to give my whole heart to you. I want to throw myself before you. What do you want me to do? How can I get to know you?

I want to pour my heart out to you Father. I surrender all that I have to you. I want to learn to spend quality time with you. If I communicate with you, you will communicate with me. Father, help me to remember that I am helpless without you. Take all of me Lord. Send your Holy Spirit to help me develop a relationship with you. Speak to me through your word. I surrender myself to you, Jesus. Take over my life. I want to get to know you better. I want to abide with you. Salvation is with you Lord. If I abide with you and stay with you, I will be in a saving relationship. I have to maintain this relationship through faith, prayer and the Holy Spirit.

Amen

A Perfect Rose

Have you ever taken time to really look at a rose? God made it perfect —
every petal is just right. Well, if God took so much time to make a rose perfect,
wouldn't you think that God would do so much more to make sure that man and
woman would be the most perfect human beings that He could make? God
Himself bent down and made man after His own likeness and woman was made
from man. Both were perfect. Even the world was perfect before sin entered
into the world. A baby, when it comes into the world, is perfect. It has all of its
little fingers and toes but it is so small. Oh what a wonderful miracle to behold.
And when you hold this small baby, it reminds you of the rose when it first
"peeks" up. It is closed and very, very small. The baby after it is fed, nurtured,
taught right from wrong and the love of Jesus, grows into a bright and beautiful
child. Now with more feeding, nurturing and teaching, the child becomes a
teenager and finally an adult. That reminds me of the rose after being full grown
and taken special care of, now stands tall and its petals are open wide and so
beautiful.

Now you are all grown up. You stand at the crossroads of life and think,
"which way should you go?" LEFT OR RIGHT? What choices do you have?
Well, if you choose Jesus, He has already proven Himself. He died on the cross
for our sins. Just give Him the chance to show you how much He loves you.
From the moment you lay down to sleep to the minute you wake up, 'JESUS IS
THERE!" When you go about your daily routine, 'JESUS IS THERE!" When
you sit down for your meals, "JESUS IS THERE!" If you have a family, 'JESUS
IS THERE!" If you don't have a family, Jesus has promised to be that family for
you. When you are ill and it doesn't seem that you will get well, "JESUS IS
THERE!" If you are in a situation you just can't see how you can get out of it,
'JESUS IS THERE!". Whatever you do, wherever you go, Jesus is there with
you. Just call on His holy name, J.E.S.U.S. He promises you that inner peace.
That means whatever happens in your life He will go with you. Learn to pray to
your Father who is in Heaven. Read His word. Talk to Him as your friend, your
best friend. He told us that He would be with us to the end if we turn our lives
over to Him. And, as He has promised, in His Father's house is many mansions.
He will come again and take us home to live with Him (John 14: 1-4).

Sometimes we feel that we don't have anything in life. We feel that no one
loves us and we are all alone. Always remember your Heavenly Father is always
there and the way He cares for the rose that is always perfect. He loves and cares
for us much, much more. Put trust always in your Heavenly Father who is
waiting for you with open arms. Now your second choice is Satan. What does
he have to offer? Just like he deceived Eve in that beautiful garden (Gen. 2), he
is there to do you the same way. He will show you that living with someone who

is not your mate is "the thing to do in the 90's", that stealing is an "art" and, if you get away with it, you are good. He'll convince you that being on drugs is cool — you know you have to "go with the flow". He tells them that everyone that has made something of themselves is on some type of drugs, and don't let anyone tell you that they are not. You listen to Satan and, all of a sudden, you get caught stealing or are with someone else's mate, or you are hooked on drugs. Then everything starts going downhill. Where is your pal, Satan, who gave you all of that advice? Is he there for you? NO! Does he care? NO! You now feel so all alone you are either in jail, thrown in the street and with no place to go.

Satan is nowhere to be found. He thinks he already has you "hooked". He is somewhere laughing at you because you feel that you have no hope.

Always remember how much Jesus loves you and He is there waiting for you with open arms. Let Him in. He will clean you up and turn your life around. THANK THE LORD!

A ROSE

R   is the rejoicing in Heaven when one of His little ones who was lost is found

O   Oh one day we shall behold Him face-to-face. Only the righteous will be with God.

S   My Saviour freed me one day out of Satan's grips and now I can sing the song "How Great Thou Art".

E   Eternal life will I have because I gave my life to Christ.

Hallelujah!

FOR GOD SO LOVED THE WORLD THAT HE GAVE HIS ONLY BEGOTTEN SON THAT WHOSOEVER BELIEVED IN HIM SHALL NOT PERISH BUT HAVE EVERLASTING LIFE.

John 3:16

I Have Overcome

As I now think back on my life I was a "disturbed" child, but I never had the courage to talk to anyone about the way I felt, how lonely and alone I felt. I had a hollow place in my heart, a place that had never been filled. I think that one of the worst feelings in the world is to feel that no ones loves you. I did not live with my younger brothers and sisters but I would go and visit with them some of the time. When I would visit my younger brothers and sisters, one of my sisters thought that I was just the girl next door. She didn't know that I was her older sister.

As a small child I was told by my grandmother that I was not loved by my parents. I was also told that I was quite ill when I was very young and my parents didn't have the time to care for me. I was a child and, of course, I believed whatever was said to me. I was told stories about my childhood time after time and, each time afer I was told these stories, I would sink deeper and deeper into myself. I never had the courage to ask any questions. I didn't even ask my grandmother any questions after she would talk to me. I would just go to my room and cry. I would ask God why they didn't love me. After all, I was one of their children too. But my heart was left to yearn. My grandmother had a little money and she tried to keep up a good front for the neighbors. We all went to church every Sabbath. We would get all dressed up, giving the neighbors the impression that we were the ideal Christian family. They were always hugging and kissing, telling each other that they loved one another. My family didn't know how to love.

Although I attended church each week, I didn't know Jesus Christ for myself. I was told that God would send me someone to love. That was the only hope that I had. I thought to myself, one day I will find someone to love me. But it never happened. I went year after year with no one who loved me in my life. While my friends were announcing that they were in love and getting married, I kept wishing that it would be me. I was always a "good" girl. I would never disobey my elders, but good things never seemed to come to me.

As I became an adult, I found myself just as lonely as I was as a child. I have now learned that sometimes we take matters into our own hands and then we want to blame God for our mistakes. God is not the one who sends trouble into our lives – Satan does and he knows just how to get us. Have you heard the old folks' saying, "you jump out of the frying pan into the fire"? Well, that is just what happened one night. I got into a "situation" and I became pregnant. Of course I had to tell my parents, and my grandmother was the first to put me out of her home. My parents were not too pleased to have me with them. As I reflect now, I realize I didn't have the courage then to take control of my own life. I could have made a way for me and my baby. But being an obedient young woman, I still did as I was told.

I married this man who was much older than I was. I didn't love him and he didn't love me. He made my life a living hell. We had an apartment. I was there alone, pregnant and with no money. But what was so pitiful was I was never taught how to survive in the real world. I did finish high school but I had no skills to fall back on, so I was at his mercy. Whatever he did, I accepted. After nine months, I went into labor. It was a hard "draw out" time – about thirty-seven hours. I was blessed with a beautiful little baby boy. As I looked into his little face, nothing else seemed to matter. I had someone who needed me. As soon as I got used to taking care of this little baby, I found myself pregnant again and, eleven months later, I found myself pregnant for the third time. It seemed as though I was digging myself deeper and deeper into a marriage with no way out. I now had three babies. How could I take care of all of these small children? I now felt alone again. I was home all of the time taking care of my three children. I never left them alone. I was with them morning to night. The only thing I had to look forward to was crying babies, a run-down apartment, and no future. No one knew what I was feeling.

Although I would visit my family once in a while, they didn't know the depth of my pain and sorrow. Sometimes my sisters would help me with my children; they would even spend the night and we would have a cookout or just talk half of the night. I used to really enjoy their company. About two years later, I found myself pregnant again. I would just cry and, sometimes, I would ask God "Why me Lord, Why me!" I was always an obedient child. I tried to do what I was told but I was in trouble again, and it seems that all I had was my children and, to my disbelief, these children really loved me and they needed me. I might not have received the love I needed from a mate or from family, but I had my children. They were a handful, but they were mine. Now my days and nights were full because, by the time I would put my children to bed, I would be so tired that the only thing that I felt like doing was taking a hot bath and just "relaxing". I didn't have time for any outside activity. Of course, what I called "relaxing" was probably more like a state of emotional shock.

I could see so many good things happening in the lives of the girls I had grown up with. They had good husbands, were buying new homes, and some of them had blooming careers. I would feel so badly when I would see them because I felt that I had nothing. But, at that time, I could never have known that I had the best gift of all – I had my children. I had someone to love me. The children were getting bigger and I could get out with them. The baby was now two and the rest of them could do a lot of things for themselves. I thought I was finished having babies. I had two boys and two girls and, one day, I found out that I was pregnant again. The only thing I could say was, "not again Lord, not again! My God, what am I to do?!" I didn't want to tell anyone since I didn't believe in abortions. I was "stuck" again. I did love my children. I just didn't want anymore. I wanted to raise the children that I had and do something with my life. But now I found myself pregnant again. This was my fifth pregnancy.

I felt as though my life had just hit "rock bottom". But, to my surprise, this pregnancy was not as bad as before. I started getting bigger and bigger. When I was in my ninth month, a day before my due date, I found out that I was giving birth to twins and that they would be born at any time now. I was so nervous that I was shaking all over. I couldn't believe it. Was I becoming a baby machine? Now I am having them two at a time! "Lord, what was I going to do with two more babies?!" I already had four small children. Now I am about to give birth to twins. Now I had a child in school all day, one in school half-a-day, two toddlers running around the house, and two infants to care for. I would take my children to church. I tried to keep them dressed nice but, through it all, I didn't really give my life over to the Lord. I think I blamed God for what was happening in my life.

My mother started coming over and would talk, but we never did discuss what was on my mind. I never had the courage to ask her about what I was thinking, or tell her just how I felt about my life. She became very ill and then she died – and I never did find out what I wanted to know. Soon after her death, my grandmother died and, three years later, my father died. So there was no one else to ask. Just as I have done all of my life, I pushed that part of my life deep down in my mind as I always did. My children were now becoming older and older. They were no longer little infants. They were all in school and I found myself a job. At first it was just a part-time job but I was starting to learn how to survive. One thing men forget is babies don't stay babies forever. They do grow up. After I had worked for a few years, I moved out taking my six children and starting a new life for us all. It was very hard. By this time my children were getting out of hand – although I surely used to pray to God. But I didn't make Him a part of our lives. We said our prayers and we would say our blessings before we ate, but we didn't put Christ first in our lives like we should have.

I know that I was not a perfect mother to my children. We had to learn to love each other and to help each other, and I think that we now have a wonderful relationship with each other. I think, through the years, my children knew that I would do anything to help them and I would stick with them "through thick and thin". It took me many, many years and many, many mistakes to get my life in harmony with God. Many family members said that my children would end up in jail, on drugs, or that they were just no good. Well it seems that the Lord just reached out and put His precious arms around us and steered us right back into His fold. They made many mistakes. So did I. But God was there with us. He has always been there with us. I think that we all learned from our mistakes.

When we didn't have food in the house, God would send someone to help. When we didn't have a place to live, God never let us be outside with no place to live. God never left our side. We left Him. Jesus really loves us and He was always with us. Although I had a hard life and thought no one loved me, Jesus taught me how to love. He promised me that, if I would put Him first in my life, He would never forsake me all the days of my life. And I took Him at His word. I now know the Lord as my personal Savior. He has bought me a mighty long way.

"THANK YOU JESUS FOR THE PRECIOUS GIFT OF ALL MY WONDERFUL CHILDREN AND, NOW, ALL *OF* MY BEAUTIFUL GRANDCHILDREN. AT LAST, I CAN SAY WITHOUT A DOUBT IN MY MIND: **I HAVE OVERCOME**".

Knock, Knock

The first of the month, twelve months in the year, in your beautiful complex there is a knock at your door. The voice you hear is your "so-called friend". Have you ever stopped to think how this man could be a friend? Does he ask how you are? How your children are? Does he ask if you need a little money to last during the month? But your friend has the nerve to ask you if you need him. What does he mean when he asked you do you need him? Have you ever stopped to figure out what he is asking you? I don't think so. He comes to you with his little bags of so-called "goodies". And you feel so good and so happy to see him. You can't wait for the mailman to come. You don't even have time to feed your children before he comes. The way the drugs make you act is what he is living for because the more you need it, the more you will buy.

After a while you have spent your whole check. What about your rent, your children's clothes, food and pampers? Remember you only get one check a month. What do you do now? First you sell anything that you can in your house. Just like that check isn't yours. I'm sure you brought the furniture in your home with your children's money. So you wouldn't have that money if it wasn't for your children. So you don't have the right to do whatsoever you want to with the check. So when your friend comes you sell the t.v., v.c.r, the stereo. He even takes your children's food stamps. You will sell your own body for the drugs. You will even do all types of things for the drugs. You will steal to get the money for drugs. I know sometimes you feel there is no turning back, and the only thing you have on your mind is to get money for the next high. What is so bad, you and your friends don't have a mind of your own. You all just follow one another. Not one of you have the courage to say "No!" and not care what the rest of your friends think. And you can't depend on a man to change you. You have to depend on yourself and what to change. This is what is bad about C.R.A.C.K.

C is for the crack you are willing to put into your body to drain you of your health and strength. It takes you from your little babies and you don't think children know the difference. You lose your home and everything you have.

R is for that rock-like substance you spend every penny you have and don't care at that time who suffers for it.

A is for the aggravation you go through after you are sober and find out how much you have lost.

C   is for the crimes you are willing to do to get the drugs.
K   is for the fact that it will kill you if you keep it up.

I have heard all about your friend who comes around, only when you have money.

Now I want to tell you about a real friend who is always there. I know a real friend. He won't rip you off and leave you alone. He loves you so much, and He is so sad when you let Satan fool you into taking drugs. One of my favorite Bible verses is Philippians 4:13, "I can do all things through Christ which strengthen me". If you read your Bible and really believe that Christ is on your side, you can do anything. He will give you the strength you need. Ephesians 6:11 says, "Put on the whole armour of God that ye may be able to stand against the wiles of the devil". To put on the whole armor, you must study for yourself. Don't worry about what your other friends may say about you. Learn by God's help to be a leader instead of a follower. Matthew 5:16 says, "Let your light so shine before men that they may see your good works and glorify your Father which is in heaven". How can your Light shine when you are doing the devil's will? Matthew 7:7 tells us, "Ask, and it shall be given to you; seek, and ye shall find; knock, and it shall be opened to you".

When you learn to love the Lord with all your heart and soul, you will be surprised at the inner peace you will have. No more guilt feelings. Just ask the Lord. Don't wait! Start now! Seek Him in His word. Study everyday. Knock and it will be given to you. Trust Jesus! Don't wait until you hit rock bottom to find Him. Start now! Right now! John 3:16 clearly says, "For God so loved the world that He gave His only begotten son that whosoever believeth in Him shall not perish but have everlasting life. God sent His only Son to die for the world. Do you think for a moment Jesus wanted to die? Matthew 26:39 says Jesus prayed, "My Father, if it be possible let this cup pass from me nevertheless not as I will but as thou will". You see, Jesus prayed to his Father when He was on this earth.

He didn't want to die but He was doing His Father's will. He had to die to save us. So every time we sin we open the wounds in Jesus' feet and hands. So the next time your "so-called friend" asks you if you need him, tell him you no longer need his fake high. We have Christ – a real friend, someone who loves us so much He was willing to die on His cross for me. Matthew 6:21 tells us, "For where your treasure is there your heart is also". When you spend your time getting high, running to bars and thinking you are having a good time, that's where you treasure is. Your heart is there also. In Revelation 3:20, "Behold I stand at the door and knock. If any man hears my voice and opens the door I will come in and sup with him and he with me". Through your conscience, the Holy Spirit can speak to you. And if you pray and study and get to really know Jesus, He will come into your heart and comfort you.

In Mark 11:22-23 Jesus answering saith unto them, "Have faith in God for verily I say unto you that whosoever shall say unto this mountain be thou removed, and be thou cast into the sea and shall not doubt in his heart but shall believe that those things which he saith shall come to pass: He shall have whatsoever he saith". So if you only have faith in God, you can move mountains. You can remove that obstacle that can get in your way to keep you from seeking Christ. Just give him a chance. You have tried everything else and made a mess out of your life, let Jesus pick up the pieces. TRY JESUS!

T   Trust in the one who was willing to die for you.

R   Rest your weary head on His shoulders. He will comfort you.

Y   If you want a change in your life (TRY JESUS!)

J   Jesus is your rock. Trust Him. He will never let you down.

E   Every time you truly pray to the Father He will answer you.

S   Surrender your heart to the Lord and see the big difference.

U   Unless you put on the whole armor of God, you cannot resist man who knocks on your door and asks if you need him.

S   Seek Jesus when you find yourself wanting to do the will of Satan.

Love

Love is one of the simplest words in the world. It means just what it says — L.O.V.E. God told us to love the Lord thy God with all thy heart and with all thy soul and with all thy mind. Thou shall love thy neighbor as thyself (Matt. 22: 37-39). In this world, we use these words so freely (I LOVE YOU). Do you really know the meaning of the word (LOVE)? Look it up in the dictionary. It says, "a deep and tender feeling of fondness and devotion". I guess we learned to use the words from our parents and grandparents (I LOVE YOU).

We hug and kiss one another and say, "I love you", with never ever giving the words any thought at all. The next time you see a loved one coming and you get ready to greet them, before you let the words come out of your mouth (I LOVE YOU) think about this — what do I really think of this person? What lies have I told someone about this loved one and how have I taken advantage of their goodness? How can you look this person in the face after all you have done to them? And yet you smile in their face and say those words (I LOVE YOU). But when a person is really sincere, truly loves the Lord, and is willing to do all they can do to help someone when they are in need, you will not hear them talk about all they have done to help you — at any point. This loved one is sincere and, when they say (I LOVE YOU), it is so comforting and soothing because their love comes from the heart.

I wish everyone would really know what real love means. God loves us so much that He gave His only begotten Son to die for us so we might be saved. Love does not mean that you can say anything to hurt the loved one. You might even go so far as to tell your children all types of lies on your loved one. Oh how sad because someday the child is going to learn the truth about this person that you are trying to put down. What you are attempting to do is put yourself on a pedestal. Before you know it you have done so much "dirt" to people, and you never thought that people would find out about your wickedness.

But people, God is going to tear all the covers off of your lives and, not only will that loved one find out about your past, so will your children. You may try to cover up your past by telling your children how you were mistreated by loved ones. What you really should be telling them is how this loved one came to your defense time after time and they really didn't have to, "THAT's LOVE!" They hear time after time how you lie and stab them in the back, and they forgive you and try to forget the things you have done to them. "THAT'S TRUE LOVE!"

What you should be doing is asking God to help you to straighten out your life. And thank God for letting this loved one be in your life and your children's life because, believe it or not, your family is the only thing you have on this earth. God gave you family so you wouldn't be all alone. Stop and ask yourself how you feel when you have mistreated all of your family? How does that make you feel? You can lie to others and try to convince them that your family is all wrong and they hate you, and how they have mistreated you all of your life. But when you close the door and your conscience starts "whipping" you, your family may never know the truth — but you will.

Anytime you try to put God's people down it will backfire on you every time. God will show His people the truth about you so you might as well stop because you are the one who is alone, not your loved one. Not only does your loved one have God's love, but they have the love of other family members and they find comfort in both loves. Even when everything seems to be going all wrong in their lives, God is there for them and He gives them that inner peace and, along with God's love and the love of their families, what more could you ask.

Now it is up to you. Do you want to keep sneaking around lying, conniving, and putting loved ones down and always getting caught? Or do you want a new life? The only way you can start is by fully giving your life to Christ. One thing that is very true is that God does know your heart. He knows when you are sincere and if you want to change your life. He will be there for you and you can find that inner peace with Christ. And your family's love will be added.

"IT IS UP TO YOU. IT IS YOUR DECISION. WHAT DO YOU WANT? TRUE LOVE OR LONELINESS?"

A Still Small Voice

A STILL SMALL VOICE. Do we hear that still small voice? In our busy schedules, do we even recognize that still small voice speaking to us? The Lord is trying to speak to us. But our minds are so involved with other things, we cannot hear Him speaking to us. The Lord wakes us up each and every day of our lives. When we wake up, we seem to have a clear mind and that still small voice speaks to us and we have all kinds of thoughts going through our minds reflecting on all the good things that have happened in our lives. We thank God for all that He has done for us. And we pray and thank Him. But then we go about our busy day, never again taking a moment to stop to listen to that still small voice. We worry about all the bills that we have accumulated through the year. It happens so fast! We start off with one credit card and end up applying for others. The companies will give us all that we apply for. God gives us common sense. We can use the cards wisely or foolishly! It is all up to us now. Once we are deeply in debt and we don't see any way out, we call on the Lord to help us.

When we are about to lose everything that we have, then we start praying and listening for that still small voice — asking God for help. Even in our families, when everything is going good, we sometimes become so busy we forget to ask the Lord to come into our lives and guide and protect our families in their daily lives — until they get into trouble. Then we want everyone to pray for our child. The whole family starts praying and that's when they listen for that still small voice. Sometimes the Lord has to step back and let us receive the "knocks and bumps" from the devil. We then look up and holler, "LORD HAVE MERCY! Help us!" Then, at that moment, we think about the love of God, and we start trying to listen for that still small voice.

Our minds are so clogged up sometimes, Satan has us right where he wants us. Sometimes it is through other people. You know the ones who you thought were your friends that you will do anything in the world for? They are beautiful friends as long as they need you. But when they get on their feet again they seem to stop speaking to you, and they even seem to turn their heads the other way when they see you come by. Now, in your heart, you feel hurt. It really bothers you because now that friend or family member acts like they are better than you are. And it seems that they have more than you now that they are back on their feet. They seem to forget all the wonderful things that you have done for them — listening to their problems, trying to give them the help that they needed. Sometimes you are up with them all night, even though you are tired. You hang in there because you were needed. When you think back on all that you have done for your friend or family member and see how they are treating you, you become angry and then you think about the person over and over again —

wondering just why they have treated you this way after you have been so good to them. But the only thing you are doing is clogging up your mind, and Satan will keep things on your mind so you can't hear that still small voice.

I don't care what is going on in our mind, just turn it over to God. After all He saw what you did for that person and, although the friend or family member didn't give you the recognition that you deserved, the Lord saw what you did and He rewards you for doing it. You might not recognize what the Lord did for you but, believe me, He did something special for you because you opened up your heart and did something nice for someone else — and you didn't think about yourself. I thought about what the voice of God had told me. I put all of those thoughts aside for a while and got up from my desk where I was writing this paper and I decided to take a break. I went into the bathroom and started to brush my teeth, and that quickly Satan flashed something else in my mind to clog it up again. Listen folks, we have to learn to keep our minds on Christ at all times. Satan is like a cancer trying to get hold of you any way that he can. He wants to stop us from hearing that still small voice. It is a funny thing. Human beings are the only ones who have a hard time listening to the voice of the Lord. The only thing that the Lord had to do was to speak to the wind and the waves and they were still. The spirit will not yell at you or smack you around to get your attention. He will just speak to you in a still small voice.

THE LORD ASKS US TO BE STILL AND KNOW THAT I AM GOD (Ps. 46:10).

Who is This Man Named Jesus?

Some describe Jesus as tall and slender. His skin is white, hair is long and brown, and eyes are pictured as sky blue. Then some decided that Jesus should be black. So He is imaged as being the athletic type with dark skin, hair black either in an afro or dreadlocks, and the color of His eyes are brown. Although people pictured Jesus differently in the color of His skin, they seem to all agree on what He wore. They portray Him dressed in a long white robe with a girdle around His waist, wearing sandals on His feet and a staff in His hand. Years ago if you professed to be a Christian, your home had a picture of Jesus hanging up in your living room. He was white with long brown hair and blue eyes. We taught our children that this was a portrait of Jesus. This is the picture that we grew up with and our children thought that this was what Jesus looked like. Through the years, black people started to become aware of their blackness and someone thought that Jesus should be a black man. Now hanging in black homes is a picture of a black Jesus.

In today's society, we are like the Scribes and Pharisees were in Jesus' day. Instead of them listening to Jesus as He tried to teach them about the love of God, they were trying to find out who His parents were. They didn't want to hear what He was saying. They were more interested in knowing what Jesus' nationality was. We get all involved in the background of Jesus, and we forget about what Jesus is all about. We spend time researching books and reading documents trying to find out all we can about Jesus' background, but we don't have time to study God's word anymore or to pray to the Lord for guidance. We spend so much time in disagreeing with one another about the color of Jesus' skin or the color and texture of His hair. Sometimes, when we read about the Scribes and Pharisees, in our minds we wonder how they could have treated Jesus the way they did. But do we know who Jesus is? Just like the people then, we don't know Jesus. He has not walked on this earth in our time. But, if we really want Him to, He will come into our lives and live with us. We can live our lives so that Christ can be seen through us.

Who is this man named Jesus? Who is this Son of God? Who is this man who could come down from Heaven and enter into the womb of a virgin and become a newborn babe? Who is this man named Jesus who at a very young age could sit in with the educators and ask them questions that only an educated person could ask? Although He knew who He was, He still obeyed His earthly parents and did everything that He was told. Who is this man named Jesus who, after being baptized by John the Baptist, He stepped out of the water and heard His Heavenly Father when He said, "this is my beloved Son in whom I am well pleased". Who is this man named Jesus who, after fasting for forty days and nights, took on the devil and then the devil did all that he could to tempt Jesus but he had to leave Jesus alone because Jesus quoted scripture after scripture to the old devil. When he found out that he could not win, he left Jesus alone. Who is this man named Jesus who, after defeating the devil, went about His Father's business preaching the Gospel and choosing good men to follow Him?

Who is this man named Jesus who healed the sick of all kinds of ailments and all manner of diseases? Who is this man named Jesus who could cure people possessed with the devil and those who were insane? Who is this man named Jesus who, after seeing the multitudes, opened His mouth and began to teach them. He started with the Sermon on the Mount and he taught the people the Lord's Prayer. Who is this man named Jesus who could walk on water and command the winds and the waves to be still? Who is this man named Jesus who could restore sight to the blind, cause a man who had never walked before to take up his bed and walk? Who is this man named Jesus who took five loaves of bread and two fish and fed five thousand men, women and children? And, after dinner, the disciples gathered up twelve baskets of leftovers and later He fed four thousand. No one else could feed such a multitude like Jesus. Who is this man named Jesus who loved the people so much that He taught them in parables so that they could understand what He was trying to teach them? Who is this man named Jesus who was never out of touch with His Father which is in Heaven? Who is this man named Jesus who showed the people that the Scribes and Pharisees made the Sabbath a burden but Jesus showed the people that the Sabbath is a delight.

Who is this man named Jesus who knew that His mission here on earth was to die? He was aware that soon His life was going to end. He knew what was about to happen to Him but He trusted His Father and said, "thy will be done". Man had sinned so much, had become so wicked that God looked down and saw the terrible condition of the world. It grieved Him to know that people no longer took the time to pray. They no longer put their trust in God. So he sent His Son Jesus down in order to teach the people about the love of God. Who is this man named Jesus who came down from heaven and humbled Himself for us? He knew that people were talking about Him. He knew that they had been plotting against Him in order to kill Him. The only time the people surrounded Jesus was when He was performing miracle after miracle for them, or when He was feeding the multitude. Who is this man named Jesus who knew that He was about to be betrayed by a kiss for thirty pieces of silver, by one who had walked with Him. The other disciples fled, still another one denied Him three times, but Jesus still loved the people so much that He was willing to suffer and die that we might be saved. If Jesus had not shed His blood for us, we would never be able to reign with Christ and His Father in that beautiful Kingdom in Heaven.

Who is this man named Jesus? Who watched as the multitude picked a well-known prisoner named Barabbas to be released from prison, but the crowd would not free Jesus who was innocent of all the charges that were brought against Him.

Who is this man named Jesus who looked on as Pontius Pilate asked what he should do with Jesus? The crowd cried out, "crucify Him, crucify Him!". How sad Jesus must have felt as He saw how much the people hated Him and how much they wanted to kill Him. Who is the man named Jesus? For our sins He was mocked, spit upon and a thorn of reed was placed upon His head. He was hit in the face. He was beaten with a stick and was taken to a place called Golgotha. There, they laid Him on a cross. The nails that were driven into His hands and in His feet represent how wicked males and females had become. Jesus knew that He had to suffer and die in order for us to be saved. He had to suffer and die for our sins. He could have called on His father and He would have sent many thousands of angels to help Him but, if he did, we could never be saved.

Who is this man named Jesus who gave up His life for me and for you? He loved us so much that He laid in the tomb for three days. He rose from the grave, because no grave could hold my Jesus. After all that the people put Jesus through, He did not go back to His Father in Heaven and leave us here alone. He sent us a comforter which is the Holy Ghost. Who is this man named J E S U S? Well He is our Lord and Savior Jesus Christ. I don't worry about the color of His skin. I don't care about His nationality. The only thing that I know is Jesus loves us. Jesus gave His life for us. No one has ever loved me that much. As I read in His book, the Bible, it tells us that Jesus is the light of the world. He is our hope in the time of trouble and, with Him, all things are possible. If it wasn't for His love for us, we would be lost. Jesus, dear Jesus — how excellent is thy name. How great thou art?

This man named Jesus is there when we need Him. He has never deceived us. He has never left us. We can call on Him for help night or day. His line is never busy. This man named Jesus left and went back to Heaven but He has promised us that in His Father's house is many mansions and He has gone to prepare us a place. He will come back to receive us unto Himself. One day we will look up and into the sky, and we will see this man named Jesus coming back for us. At that moment we will not care about who He is or where He comes from. The only thing we will care about is that He has come back for us.

I Shut My Eyes and Imagine That I Was Touching the Face of God

I have made some very serious mistakes in my life in the past before I really developed a beautiful relationship with God. Sometimes, in the past, I thought I was going to have a nervous breakdown or just give up and let myself go. I used to blame God for my troubles. I felt that, although I made a stupid move in my life, God should have sent someone to lighten the blow. Although the storm felt as though there was no end, it seemed to throw me from side to side and it felt as though I was digging a hole for myself and I was in deeper and deeper. But what I didn't realize was that God was turning my life around. At first, I didn't know it. I thought I was all alone, that He had left me. Finally, I admitted to myself that I'm the one who messed up — not God. But, in His marvelous way, he took the mess that I had made out of my life and turned it into something positive. I could have been all strung out on drugs or in jail. I could have also been dead. But I was His child and He held me in His strong arms and He never never let me go until I realized that God truly loved me.

With His love I have become stronger and stronger than I have ever been in my whole life. With God by my side, I can do anything. With Him, I can't go wrong. Sometimes we are crossing the street in the crosswalk and a car turns and he doesn't see you. God dispatches His Angel, and the Angel stands between you and the car. Or you might be driving down the highway and the car in front of you stops suddenly and you try to put on brakes fast but, just before you hit the car in front of you, God dispatches His Angel and the Angel stands between you and the car. When you are on an airplane and it seems as though you are in the Heavens itself, God holds that plane in the air.

When our children attend school — public or private — and you send God before them and they arrive safely, God has protected them through the day. When the day is over and you think back on all of the things that God has done, you sigh and say THANK YOU GOD for being so merciful to us and THANK YOU for sending your Angels to intervene in my life. I shut my eyes and imagine that God is gently smiling back at me saying, "You're welcome".

The world has become so wicked it is hard to see God's face. But He is there for us now and always, and the only thing that we have to do is to pray and ask Him to come into our lives. He is waiting and watching for us to remember that He is our Heavenly Father and also to remember that, not only did He make us, He gave His only Son to die for our sins so we might have a chance to be saved. He loves us that much! In the beginning, when the world was fresh and new, God would come down and walk with the new man and woman that He had made. Everything was perfect and so beautiful! They probably had a lot of questions to ask God, and He was so patient with them. They were not afraid of God before sin entered into the world.

I can imagine that God loved to come down and spend time with Adam and Eve. We cannot see God face-to-face because of sin, but we can feel His presence in nature such as the trees. They are so big and strong, but none of them are the same. They bring forth their own fruit, and the flowers come up so beautifully and smell so good. You just know that God is here. You see the great mountains and wonder how were they formed. You feel the warm breezes of summer on your face, or you look out your window and see the picture of snow as it falls from the sky. It is so beautiful. It covers everything. It is so white and it makes you wonder where it comes from. God has a plan for everything and everyone for all that He does here on earth. He takes the time to hear the tiniest cry of His smallest child. He hears and cares for everyone.

God has no "picks" nor does He join any certain groups. Sometimes I imagine what God looks like. Is His skin light or dark? Is His hair long or short? Is He tall or short in stature? Are His eyes light or dark? Then I look around and I can see the face of God in that person who is disabled, a young girl who is pregnant, or that young person who has gone astray. I can also see Him in that elderly person who just needs someone to talk to, or that little child whose eyes you look into as you pick it up and hold it close to your heart as it cries. When you look into the face of your fellow man, you see the face of God.

When Christ is in your life you can't help being kind to others. It just comes naturally. Everyone might not love you; some might talk about you. But, remember, when Jesus walked this earth He did all that he could to help EVERYONE. But some turned ON HIM. Some talked about him. Some wanted him dead. So if they would do this to the Lord when He was here on this earth, what makes us think that the world would treat us any differently!

Sometime I break God's commandments — especially about the Sabbath. I don't mean to but, sometimes, I am out on Friday and the sun sets before I can get home or I am not finished taking care of my business before the Sabbath comes in. Since you have come into my life, I never want to disobey you Father. I never want YOUR FACE to be hidden from me. In the end, as we stand before God, we will be standing so tall and excited about meeting God and His precious Son, Jesus, at last. We will look like a beautiful rainbow of colors. All have waited so long to see our Heavenly Father face-to-face. He has waited so long for us to be with Him. He has been preparing beautiful mansions in Heaven just for us.

On this earth God has nurtured us, watered us, and protected us so patiently, so gently. Our Heavenly Father loves us so much that He stood by us all of our lives. We could always depend on the Lord. One day, as we stand before our Heavenly Father thanking Him for at last bringing us Home, we no longer have to shut our eyes to imagine touching the face of God.

NOW WE CAN REACH OUT AND TOUCH THE FACE OF GOD!

If I Could Just Touch the Hem of His Garment

She stood watching this wonderful man as He passed by her. He was going about His work healing the people. He also preached to them as they gathered around them. She thought to herself, "I wonder if I get closer to Jesus could He help me?" She had been sick with an issue of blood for twelve years. No earthly doctor could help her. If she could only get close to Him. I know that she was just a lonely poor lady because she had paid all of her money out to doctors to make her well. She knew that she had to move fast because Jesus was moving on through the crowd and she didn't want to miss Him. So she decided to rush past Him and just touch the hem of His garment. He would never know who touched Him, but she had enough faith to believe that if she could just touch Him she would be made well. With all of the people pressing against Jesus, He felt someone touching Him. He stopped and asked, "Who touched me?" At that very moment the woman looked up at Jesus and He said to her, "Daughter be of good comfort. Your faith hath made you whole". Jesus is the only one who could have made the woman well.

The woman had faith. She had heard of the miracles that Jesus had performed and she believed that if she could just touch the hem of His garment she would be healed. The issue that the world has passed on from generation to generation, from country to country is called sin. Satan is the author of sin and he has been deceiving people for centuries. He has a way of convincing people that they don't need Jesus, the Bible is old fashioned, and faith is an Old Testament belief. He convinces people to put their faith in therapists and psychologists who also are human beings and have faults of their own. So the cycle continues. The issue of sin gets larger and larger and wider and wider until the world is becoming so corrupted it feels like the world just can't touch the hem of His garment anymore. It feels like Satan is "dimming the lights" on the world and people are just stumbling around in the dark. He knows that he has just a short time so he is trying to snatch as many people as he can. He doesn't care if they are young or old; if they are children or teens. He doesn't discriminate. He accepts them all.

It is so easy for us to believe a lie. People all over the world are trying to find the faith that they need to carry on. Satan puts it into people's minds that they should go to the ends of the earth looking for the faith that they need to go on with their lives. He makes them believe that if they would put their faith in this statue of a person that has been dead for centuries they can make everything alright in their lives. People pray to them. They will kiss the statue, kneel before it in reverence, and will pay any amount of money just to have the opportunity to get a glimpse of this miracle that could never happen.

Everyone is looking for that miracle. Everyone needs faith in their lives, but no one wants to reach out and touch the hem of His garment. Satan tries to make life so confusing and complicated, and people believe him because it is easier for people to believe a lie rather than the truth. That issue that the world faces is called sin. It moves into the hearts and minds of men and women and causes them to become weak. They don't know how to love one another. The only thing that they have in mind is trying to make that almighty dollar. Nothing else seems to matter. They don't have time for their children. Some just don't remember how to call upon the Lord. Sin winds its way into our children's lives. They don't have any respect for themselves or their parents or anyone else. The teenage boys are dead before they are fourteen years old. They are killing each other. The teenage girls are mothers before they are old enough to go to high school. Small children are carrying guns and are not afraid to use them on anyone who gets in their way. Drugs are a way of life now. There is so much sickness, and diseases are being diagnosed so fast that doctors don't have any idea what to call them or how to cure them. Death is the only cure that you have.

Satan has the world so confused and it seems that the world can't see it. Adults, children and teens go about their lives like nothing is wrong. Satan thinks that he has the world right where he wants it. The whole world is so vulnerable they cheer and applaud when they hear our leaders crying, "peace, peace!" But my Bible tells me when they cry "peace, peace" — sudden destruction comes (1 Thes. 4:3). We feel that there is not much more that can happen to this world today. Satan has really ruined everything. It seems that the world just doesn't have any hope. It feels like we are all alone. The world has forgotten that the Lord died for them centuries ago. The world thought then that they had no hope. Satan thought then that he had won but, to his surprise, he lost. When the Lord died and rose from the grave, we realized that we serve the risen Savior. The world has forgotten who Jesus is. We have forgotten that He is the Prince of Peace, that he is Alpha and Omega, The beginning and the end (Rev. 22:13).

Just like the woman who had the issue for twelve long years, she had the faith. She believed that if she would just reach out and touch the hem of His garment she would be made well. People today are looking for that great big miracle. One that they can go on the talk shows and talk about. Or one that they may be able to write a bestseller about how God sent down that big miracle to change their lives. You don't have to swim to the ends of the earth to find the Lord. You don't have to walk through fire to find Him. You don't have to charm snakes or cut yourself to get to know Him. God doesn't require that of us. The woman just reached out and touched the hem of His garment. That was so simple. She had found that faith, that pure simple humble faith in the Lord — nothing else. The Lord tells us that we can do anything if we only have the faith of a mustard seed. With just a small mustard seed we could remove mountains

(Mark 11:22-24). When Jesus felt the woman touch His garment, He knew that she had faith in Him. If the world would just believe in Jesus and believe that He is the son of God, that would be all that we needed in our lives today. Jesus is the answer to the world today. One thing about Jesus is that He will never get old or stale. He is the same yesterday, today and as long as there is a world.

ALL YOU HAVE TO DO IS TO JUST REACH OUT AND TOUCH THE HEM OF HIS GARMENT (Matt. 9:20-22; Mark 5:25-34; Luke 8:43).

I Stand at the Door and Knock

In the Living Bible, Revelation 3:20-21says:

[20]Look I have been standing at the door and I am constantly knocking. If anyone hears me calling him and opens the door, I will come in and fellowship with him and he with me.

[21]I will let every one who conquers sit beside me on my throne, just as I took my place with my Father on his throne when I had conquered.

Jesus is waiting so patiently for us to remember that He is standing at the door of our hearts knocking and asking for us to just let Him in. Sometimes the Lord is there knocking and pleading, day after day, year after year. You might "peep" out and tell the Lord "not now Lord, not now!". Some of us say, "I am in school and I have a lot of living to do. I will feel left out if I give my heart to you now and all of my friends are having a ball. I will be stuck in church with all of the 'old folks'!". Others think, "I have too much living to do right now. Later on I will give my life to you when I am older!". Or there are those who lament, "Lord I know that what I am doing is wrong, but I am in love right now and I can't let them go. I know what you are telling me is right but, as soon as I am free, I will let you in!". Sometimes we get involved in drinking alcohol or taking drugs so we can find that love that we need.

But all that you have to do is answer that little knock. It grieves the Lord when we make all kinds of excuses for not loving and trusting Him. He is still there taking care of us, even though we treat Him so badly. If we don't trust God we always get ourselves in trouble. Sometimes when we hit "rock bottom" we might remember that small voice pleading with you to just let Him in. Now, you have tried everything else. TRY JESUS! Once you give your heart to Jesus, you will never have to worry again about whether or not you have that inner peace — even though you might have all kinds of troubles in your life. Your wife or husband might not love you. Your children might not respect you but, as long as you have the love of Jesus in your heart and you take your wife, husband or your children to the altar, you will see a big difference in their lives.

God loves us so much that He gave His only begotten Son that whosoever believed in Him shall not perish but have everlasting life (John 3:16). In these last days, if we never took the time to listen to the Lord's plea for salvation before, it should be now with all of the prophecies being fulfilled all around us. When we read Revelation, we know that the time is near. Parents are raping and killing children. Children are being disrespectful to their parents. All we see around us is violence, sex and drugs in our television shows, our movies and even in the music that we listen to. People are so quick to use the Lord's name in vain. They have the nerve to curse the precious name of God whenever they want to. When things get bad for them they are the first ones on their knees asking God for help, pleading with the Lord to intervene, begging the Lord to help them through life's many, many problems.

When you are angry, how could you curse God? You should be praising His pecious name day and night. After all, He is the one who has taken care of us from the day that we were born until now. He watches over us whether we serve Him or not. The Lord could have made us so that we would do whatever He wanted us to do. But He didn't want to force us to trust Him. He wanted us to love Him and believe in Him as your Lord and Savior Jesus Christ. If you love Him, then you will keep God's commandments — all of them. You wouldn't think of telling the Lord that you would rather keep another day for His Holy Sabbath Day. You need the love of Jesus in your heart. If you truly have the love of Jesus in your heart scripture tells us, "I can do all things through Christ which strengthens me" (Philippians 4:13).

Christ is everything to me. If you truly love Him then you will never doubt God's word and you would never be ashamed to tell others about the love of God. Read His word each and every day. Talk to the Lord in prayer all the time. That's the only way that you will keep your eye on the Lord. Learn to depend on the Lord for yourself. He will never forsake you.

Always remember that the Lord is standing there knocking at the door of your heart. Don't make any more excuses. Run! Don't walk! Swing open the doors of your heart and let the Lord come in!

His Eye is on the Sparrow

As I sit here listening to a song, "His Eye in on the Sparrow," I am reminded it was an old favorite of my grandmother. Thoughts started running through my mind about the love of Christ and how good He has been to me and my family all of these years. I would feel guilty the times that I would go to church because, in my heart, I knew I was doing things that were not right with God. So I stopped going. I told myself, "When I got my life straightened out I would be back. But not now." That was my excuse. I put it out of my mind and didn't attend church for many years. One morning, a few years later, I was on my way to work about 6:30 in the morning. It had snowed the night before and, as I came out of my apartment, it was very cold and very dark. I didn't see anyone on the street that morning. I warmed up my car, said my usual prayer asking God to send His angel to guide and protect me on my way to work. So I turned on my radio and left for work.

I got over in the right lane and all of a sudden I hit a patch of ice, and it threw me from the end lane to the middle lane. Back and forth I went. I couldn't touch the wheel. I had no control of the car. It was like I wasn't there. The car was on its own. I thought it was going to stop. The car made a buzzing sound, and lifted itself off of the ground and threw me down a hill. The car was in mid-air. I thought I was going to die. I cried out, "Oh God, have mercy on me!" The car stopped right in front of a tree. Two men who had been watching came to my rescue and helped me out of the car. I was not hurt. Neither was my car damaged (thank you Jesus!). His eyes were on the sparrow that morning and He reminded me that He was still on the throne. I went home. I cried and prayed. I asked God to help me get my life in order.

But why? Why do we wait until we get in trouble to call on the Lord. Although we put Jesus "on the back burner", say our prayers in the morning and evening and bless our food before we eat, we don't give Him another thought during the day as we go about our daily routine. But the Lord is so good and kind to us even though we treat Him lukewarm. Jesus lets the rain pour water on the just as well as the unjust. His eye is on the righteous as well as the unrighteous. He takes care of the good as well as the bad. It hurts Him that we disobey and treat Him just like He is a stranger.

I saw an old friend of mine. We used to attend church together a long time ago. I was telling him how Jesus was back in my life again and how good it felt to be to back in church working for the Lord. I invited him to church on Sabbath. He smiled and told me, "Not now. I'm not ready to give my life to Jesus. Jesus knows that I love Him. He knows that I will be back when I stop living the way I do. He knows my heart. He understands me." We hugged each other and went separate ways. After he left, I started thinking about what he had said. I imagine his conscious was pretty clear. He had a good excuse for not turning his life over to Jesus right now. I felt kind of sad because we all do Jesus the same way at one time or another. We seem to lose sight that Jesus is the only one with His loving arms spread out to welcome us home. He is the only one who bled and died for our sins so that we may have a chance to be saved.

**HIS EYE IS ON THE SPARROW
AND I KNOW HE'S WATCHING ME!**

God Loves You

When we come into the church and take our stand, we are told that God loves you and wants you to become a Christian. Because God loves you, the church members love you also. We smile at each other and hug one another, but do we really love each other? Well, as long as that person does all the right things, they are alright with the church. But what happens when the person makes a mistake? It seems that we are more interested in what the world thinks about the church rather than what we can do to help the person in need. Instead of the church board meeting and listening to the pastor recommending what disciplinary action should be taken against this person, when we hear of a person in trouble we should first go to the individual, hug them, let them know you love them and, most of all, tell them how much Jesus loves them. Next, fall on your knees and pray. Now is the time for the Prayer Band to come in. Go on a fast for our sister or brother. Talk to this person. Listen to this person. They have a lot to say. Read to them about the love of Christ and how they can find comfort in God. Then, for more strength, read what Jesus did in the same situation.

The Scribes and Pharisees brought Jesus a woman accused of adultery. Now Jesus could have handled the situation one of two ways. He could have said I have to give this woman some type of disciplinary action so the people around will know what we stand for. But there was another choice Jesus had. He stooped down and, with His finger, wrote on the ground all of their sins. And, as they kept talking to Jesus, He kept writing one by one. They read their sins that were written on the ground. After that, they left and didn't say anything else (John 9). What do you think would happen if, while we were trying to decide what length of time we should give a person for their mistakes, a hand would appear from nowhere just like in the story of King Belshazzars and write down all of our mistakes and sins — both great and small. Would we be as quick to vote on someone else? "NO, I DON'T THINK SO!"

We need to stop and think just what we are doing and make sure that it is what Jesus wants us to do. And if we make this choice to put a person out of church, it is your responsibility to help this person to return to church. I'm not saying that we should turn our back on sin. "NO, NEVER!" But the way we go about it bothers me. We have to learn to really care and love our church family. Let's say it was our children, parents, brothers or sisters. Would we be so quick to bring them before the church board? I believe we would sit them down, talk to them and show them how they have sinned before God. We will pray for them time and time again. We would call the Prayer Band to pray and ask the Lord to intervene in our family's lives. that's the way we should treat one another — just like it was one of our very own family members. Preachers, teachers, deacons and deaconesses, ushers and all Christians stress LOVE, MUCH LOVE. We all need to learn how to love more. Do we really believe in prayer? Do we believe that prayer can change things? Well, let's stop talking prayer and love. LET'S PUT IT TO THE TEST!

Religion

At a very early age most of us are taught about Jesus and His love. Some of us are taught to recite the books of the Bible from Genesis to Revelation. Some really study and pray and know why they follow Jesus for themselves. Others follow him through tradition or because someone else told them about Jesus. The ones that study God's word and learn to pray and have developed a special relationship and know the Lord for themselves are like a man who dug deep, built a house, and laid the foundation on a rock. When the flood arose, the stream beat heavily upon that house and could not shake it for it was founded upon a rock. But the ones who followed him through tradition or by believing what they had heard about Jesus, without studying for themselves, are like a man who built a house without a foundation upon the earth against which when the stream did beat heavily against it, it immediately fell and the ruin of the house was great (Luke 6:48-49). Some call our Heavenly Father God, others call him Yahweh, and there are those who call him Jehovah. Some call his blessed son Jesus, others call him Christ, some call him Lord and others call him Yahshua. Whatever name you choose to call our Heavenly Father and His blessed son, "Praise them". Keep on calling upon them. Keep on learning about them.

There are so many different religions in the world and each has their own belief. Each one believes their way is right. Which religion should we choose? Let's turn to our Bible for help. Jesus tells us that the commandments say that we should love the Lord thy God with all thy heart and with all thy soul and all our minds and all thy strength. This is the first and greatest commandment (Matt. 22:36-40; Mark 12:29-31; Luke 10:27).

That means, if we are to follow Jesus, we are going to have to keep all of the things that God commands us to do. He tells us to keep all of his commandments — not just some. We don't mind keeping the ones that are convenient to keep. We are instructed to give all to the glory of God. If the religion that we choose doesn't keep all of God's commandments, we know that we are in the wrong one. Because we love Him with all our heart, our soul and our minds we will always put him first in our lives.

After Jesus told us which one was the greatest commandment, He then told us what was the second. He said we should love thy neighbor as thyself. Who is our neighbor? He is that man sitting in the alley so drunk he doesn't even know what is going on around him. Will we pick him up? Clean him up? Give him the help that he needs? Is our neighbor that young girl who is facing motherhood and has to hear all of the whispering and seeing the staring eyes around her? She feels so ashamed and all alone. Will we be the ones who hold out our arms in love and tell her that we love her? Is my neighbor that person who is addicted to drugs and is willing to do anything to support their habit? How can I help them?

Will I do all I can to help them get the support and intervention that they need? Will we give them a meal? Will we try to get someone to come in and give them the care and love that they need to make it in life? Are my neighbors the prisoners in jails all over the state begging for someone to visit or just write ensuring them that Jesus loves them and wants them to change their lives for the better.

In the religions that I choose, do I think I am better than other people? Am I like the two men in Luke 10:30 who saw a certain man that had been beaten up by thieves and left for dead and they passed by on the other side so they wouldn't have to help. Or is the religion I choose like the Good Samaritan who saw this man half dead and came to his rescue. Not only did he take care of the man, but paid the innkeeper to give him a place to stay. Is this the compassion that Christ wants us to have for one another? Whatever we do for others with whom we come into contact each and every day, we are really doing for our Heavenly Father who is in Heaven.

In the religion I choose, I want to study and search all of God's laws. I want to make sure that I am following the Lord's way — not man's and not tradition. This can only be done by praying and asking the Lord to send the Holy Spirit to teach us all of God's ways — not just some of them. When we study something new, we must search and pray for understanding. Don't just say, "oh we don't have to keep that law anymore" and close your minds without knowing for sure. Then you will know for yourself what the Lord demands from us. He will show us in scripture word for word. Seek the answers you need ONLY from the word. When you give your life to the Lord, He will take control of it and lead you into all truths.

Where There Is God - Part I

This message that was revealed to me was given as an inspiration to show young people the danger that they are putting their young lives in when they become involved in drugs. Though I have had no personal experience with drugs, part of the story is true. It happened in different people's lives that I have spoken to and others that I know. I have researched and asked a lot of questions and have received a lot of answers.

At about 12 years old, I started drinking very heavily. My dad brought beer by the case, and he never knew that I was helping him drink it. At 13 I had a summer job working with my dad, so I could buy whatever I wanted to with no questions asked. So I would get older kids to buy beer and wine for me. After a while, I could never get enough. I would have a beer before and after dinner. At school, I would sneak wine in my locker. I had it in a glass that could not be seen through. No one ever knew that I had been drinking. I told myself I couldn't make it through the day without my drinks. I would get the older kids to buy me beer and wine by promising them that I would treat them too. So they would keep going to the store for me, and we all drank together. I would tell my folks that I would be staying at a friend's house so they wouldn't be expecting me home. I did what I wanted to. I looked older than I was so I even had a fake I.D., and could get into bars without any problem. I felt so grown up. I met older people there who treated me as an equal and we all drank together. I was having such a good time.

One night, I was at a party. I was drinking my usual drinks when a friend said, "Why dont' you have a real drink" and gave me my first drink of liquor. At first, I didn't like it because it was strong and burned going down. But, to keep up with the crowd, I had another and another drink until I passed out. When I woke up I found out that my friends had put me to bed. Oh, I had quite a headache and my stomach was so queasy. I said that I would never drink that stuff again. So I went back to my usual drinks — wine with beer on the side. But I was always willing to try something new. One day in late summer, I was offered a cigarette. I noticed that it looked different and had a funny smell, "but what the heck", I thought to myself. I took it and tried it. At first it choked me. But I was taught how to handle it. So I asked them where I could buy some of "that stuff". I was told it was called marijuana and they taught me how to roll it. And we sat around and got high together and I liked it. It made me feel so mellow and, with my wine, I had a "good high". I couldn't wait to get out of school to have me a "joint" to relax me and just mellow me out. I felt like I had no cares in the world.

Just like anything else, my body got used to the marijuana and I began not to get "the high" like I had been. I was addicted to that "high" and nothing could fill that longing for that drug. So I started looking for the latest drugs on the street. I worked and went to school, but that wasn't enough for me. My folks tried to instill in me good values in life, and I had started to save a little money for school clothes. I told my mother that I needed some money to put some clothing in layaway. That way she wouldn't know that I didn't get the clothes. And, when it was time for me to get the clothes out, I would have the money and she would never know the difference. So I took the money and found a friend of mine. He took me to a rundown house in the lower part of town. We had to walk down a long hallway. It was very dark and I was really beginning to get scared. But I thought about that "fix" and I kept on walking. Finally, we arrived at the right door.

My friend knocked on the door and, when it opened, he spoke to the man on the other side of the door. The man didn't know me so he didn't say anything to me. He just carried on a conversation with my friend. My friend told the man what I needed, so he sold us what we asked for — some cocaine.

Then we left. We went back to my friend's apartment and he showed me how to snort the cocaine. It burned my nose so badly. I tried, but I didn't like it. My nose burned and it "ran" all of the time. Sometimes I didn't know that it was running. It even made my nose bleed without warning. I told my friend that I didn't like snorting the cocaine so he suggested that I try smoking it in a pipe. I liked that much better.

We laid around getting high all that day. My friend showed me how to put the cocaine in a needle and shoot it into my veins. I was so high I didn't know where I was, how I got there, or what time it was. I was supposed to be in school. The way I felt, I couldn't even find the school. That "high" felt so good I had to get that feeling again, but I had no more money. I was flat broke and my friend, who was just as "high" as I was, was trying to show me how we could get more cocaine. So my friend told me to go home and try to get something of value at my house and he said he would do the same and we would sell them. I agreed to do that.

I looked terrible and I was shaking so badly because I needed a "fix". But cocaine is so expensive, I couldn't afford it. The "high" just doesn't last long enough. When I arrived home, my parents were not home yet, so I got a bag and put everything I could carry in the bag and left. When I arrived at my friend's house with all of my stuff, I was waiting for my friend to show me the things that were of value that we could sell. I didn't see anything, but my friend had a good excuse. I didn't even care. I just wanted the drugs. I just wanted it! So my friend went with me to sell my parents and my belongings. I had to take any price I could. I think the pawn shop owner thought that we stole the stuff anyway. But, at this point, I didn't even care. I took whatever he gave me and went to the drug dealer's house to buy some more cocaine. We didn't have quite enough money. My friend tried to get the man to give us some credit. The man wasn't very comfortable with me being there anyway, but he didn't fall for the story my friend was trying to convince him of. He didn't give us the credit but he said, "I tell you what I will do for you". We listened so earnestly because we wanted a "fix". We didn't care what he was talking about as long as we got "the stuff".

At this time, he introduced us to crack cocaine. He told us it was a lot cheaper and I could afford it. I said, "We'll take it!" So my friend and I got our stuff and left. We went back to my friend's apartment. I was afraid to pull "the stuff" out until we were behind closed doors. I took it out of my pocket and looked at it. It looked like soap or wax, and it was cut into pieces. We took the pipe and started smoking the crack — passing it back and forth to each other. The crack made us feel so good. We had a "good high" but, after we smoked it, I started feeling so paranoid. I would smoke the crack and couldn't sit still. I would jump up every minute and look out the window looking for the police. I would sit back down, jump back up looking outside for the police. I was so scared I kept telling my friend the police were coming. I just knew that they were on their way. My friend said, "Why don't you sit down? You are making me nervous by running back and forth to that window". My friend was just the opposite. He would sit and never say a word and try to pick the spots off of the floor and furniture or in the air.

We were really some kind of pair. I would jump up all night looking out the window for the police who were not there, and my friend was trying to pick up spots off the floor and furniture that were not there. I had forgotten that I had stolen those things from the house. I didn't even care. The only thing I wanted was to feel that "high" again. I didn't know how long I had been gone. I looked horrible and I needed that "fix" so bad. I had no money. Finally, I arrived home. My parents were so frightened because they had thought the worse. My father had called the police. My mother was just crying. I didn't know what to say or what to do when I saw them. I had to make up a lie quickly, so I told them that I had been gambling and had owed some guys a lot of money and they gave me one hour to pay it back. I went on to say, "When I arrived home you were not here and I couldn't wait for you. That's why I had to take things from the house".

I gave my father the pawn ticket, and I promised them that I would never do anything like that again. They forgave me because they loved me and I had never given them a lot of trouble before. My father took the pawn ticket and got our things our of "hock". I promised them again that I would never do that to them — never.

I decided to get off of drugs. I had convinced myself that I didn't need drugs anymore. I could see the pain in my parents' faces. They had so many plans for me. They wanted me to do something with my life. I was 16 years old and failing in school. I just didn't go because I had lost interest. I just didn't seem to care about anything anymore. I used to have a job, but I didn't even call in so I guess that it was gone. I was starting to feel sorry for myself and I felt so alone. I thought about my friend and decided to go to his house.

We sat around talking about our problems but he was not interested in my problems. He was trying to get a "fix". So I started thinking of ways to get some money. I was going in with my friend to get some drugs. I convinced myself that the drugs would make me feel better, too. I remembered that I hadn't picked up my final paycheck so we borrowed a few dollars and headed out to my job. When we arrived there I found out that my father had already been there. He picked up my check and used it to pay for the things that I had "hocked". I was mad but I couldn't do a thing about it.

So we had to think of another way to get some money. I remembered old Ms. Campbell who lived in the next block. I used to do errands for her, so I told my friend to wait in the car til I got back. I knocked on the door. She was so glad to see me. We talked for a long while and I asked her if she needed anything. She told me no, so I talked and talked trying to get up enough nerve to ask for a favor. Finally, I just asked her if she could loan me fifty dollars until I received my paycheck. I promised her that I would give it back to her the next day. Because she trusted me, she gave it to me with no questions asked. I felt kind of bad knowing that I had just told a good friend a lie. But I couldn't help it. I was trying to get some drugs. We arrived at the dealer's house. The first thing he said was, "Oh, you back again!" We said, "Here, man" and gave him our money and he gave us "the stuff" and we left. We arrived back at my friend's apartment. We started smoking and smoking. We sold whatever we got our hands on and went right back to the drug dealer to buy more crack. We smoked and smoked trying to find that first "high" that we had. I was still running back and forth to the window looking for the police, and my friend was so mellow sitting quietly on the floor trying to pick the spots off the floor and the table that weren't there.

I jumped up off of the couch to run to the window when I suddenly grabbed my heart and fell back on the couch. My heart was beating so fast.

I couldn't get my breath. I broke out in a cold sweat. I couldn't move or help myself. My left side was numb. I tried to feel my face but it was numb and my mouth felt twisted. I wanted to cry out, but who would hear me! My friend was stoned so he couldn't help me. He was busy trying to catch the spots on the floor. No one could help me! No one could hear me! No one knew I was there! As I laid there on the couch, my heart was beating so fast I just knew any minute it would just stop all together. I tried to touch my face but I couldn't. My clothes were soaking wet with sweat. I just knew any minute it would be my last. I was so scared I knew that I was going to die — alone. I thought about my parents — how they loved me and how they stuck with me. And, oh, how I stole from them, lied to them, and Ms. Campbell who also trusted in me. If I had only listened to my parents I would be in school right now — not here dying. But the only one I listened to was my friend and the crack man. I used to be a nice size, now I was so small nothing fit anymore. I looked terrible. My face was all sucked in and I was starting to look so old. But I didn't care. The only thing I wanted was more drugs. I had spent everything I could get my hands on to buy drugs. I was willing to lie, steal, sell my body, anything — I didn't care. Whatever I had to do to get crack — I did it.

I wished my parents were here. I had never felt so alone. It had been a long time for me lying there and not being able to move. My heart was beating faster and faster and I couldn't move. I thought I was becoming paralyzed. The sweat was in my eyes and running down my face. I could feel myself passing out. I tried to cry out but I couldn't and, very softly I said, "Lord I don't deserve to live. But Lord, I don't want my parents to find me like this. They couldn't take it. I have hurt them enough. Please, Jesus, give me another chance. In the name of Jesus Christ I pray, Amen". I laid there for a few minutes more. Then, all of a sudden, my heart started slowing down and I could move. I got off of the couch. The first thing I said was, "THANK YOU LORD, THANK YOU!" I wiped my face. It still felt kind of numb. I went over to the phone and called my parents. They thanked God for answering their prayers and they came to my rescue right away. We prayed and cried. They even tried to help my friend. They took me to the hospital. After I was treated, they took me home. I told them how I had talked to the Lord, and I asked my parents for their help.

That night I rested in my own clean bed. You don't know how good it felt. The next day, my parents went with me to a drug rehab. My father wanted to know more about crack cocaine. He found out that some of the ingredients in crack included embalming fluid — which is a chemical to keep dead bodies from decaying fast. And also benzene — which is a clear liquid gotten from coal tar. It is a compound of carbon and hydrogen used in making varnish and dyes. He couldn't believe I was risking my life, wrecking my future for crack cocaine. I went into a drug rehab and with Christ in my life. I prayed each and every day to keep me strong. It has been a long, long time but thank God I changed so much. I used to never be able to look people in the face when I talked to them. I would look down at the ground or looked up in the air because I was so ashamed. But now, thank God, I can look you in the face and tell you how good I feel being drug-free.

One day I ran into that same friend who I used to get high with, and I was trying to show him that I was straightening out my life. I was back in school.

I attended the drug program and, best of all, I had found Christ in my life and I prayed to God every day that he kept me strong. My parents have never stopped praying for me. I have paid Ms. Campbell back her fifty dollars. And I have been doing a lot of little jobs at no charge. I am now 19 years old, and I am drug-free. I have been studying about the love of Christ all this time. I had been looking for something to give me a "charge" in life. So I chose beer, wine and liquor. Finally, drugs. Now I found Christ to fill my emptiness, and He gives me all of the boost that I need. My parents are there for me and I know that they love me. But I found out that, not only does Jesus Christ love me, but He died on the cross for me. He wants to save my soul and give me eternal life. I was running around from place to place looking for a great "high", spending all of the money that I could find. When all I had to do was to sing the praises of God and read about all His wonderful works. I talk to others who are going through what I went through. We pray together. I now help the elderly and would never think of ripping them off.

I always tell people about the love of God. I have a "high" that lasts all day long. And I didn't have to pay a cent for it. My Heavenly Father gave it to me just because He loves me and He loves you, too. If you would only trust him, He will see you through it. At one time I was running around back and forth to the "crack man". I don't need that anymore. Now I fall on my knees and talk to my Heavenly Father thanking Him for being there for me and giving me that inner peace. My goal is to help as many people as I can. That includes young women with small children who are neglecting them because of drugs. I show them that the only thing they have is their babies. I allow God to use me to help them to take care of their children, and to introduce them to God's way — not the world's way. I try to teach that young man on the street that selling drugs on the corner doesn't make him a big man. The only thing he will get is to be in jail or dead. I know that this is a big job, but I think that this is my job.

I had to reach rock bottom before I received the help that I needed. I want to spare someone else the pain and agony by trying to stop them and show them that God is real. He is there for them day and night. He loves you and He has proven it. I give out copies of the "Faith Prayer" everywhere I go. It reads.

WHERE THERE IS FAITH THERE IS LOVE
WHERE THERE IS LOVE THERE IS PEACE
WHERE THERE IS PEACE THERE IS GOD
WHERE THERE IS GOD THERE IS NO NEED

Where There is God - Part II

This message that was revealed to me was given as an inspiration to show young people the danger that they are putting their young lives in when they become involved in drugs. Though I have had no personal experience with drugs, part of the story is true. It happened in different people's lives that I have spoken to and others that I know. I have researched and asked a lot of questions and have received a lot of answers.

One day, after my regular job, I went over to the center as I did three days a week to counsel the older children and the young adults who come there for help. I told them about the alcohol and drug addiction I had as a child and young adult. I told them how I missed out on so much of my young life. I felt like I knew everything, and that I could handle the drug. I just knew that it would never get the best of me. I tell them, "Well, it almost killed me, but my parents stuck with me. They got me some help and I found Christ in my life. Now I have that inner peace that I had been looking for". I had just finished talking and praying with the young men and women there, pleading with them to stay in school and make something out of their lives, when I received a phone call. To my surprise, it was from a very dear friend of mine. We used to date some years ago. She was telling me about that big check that finally arrived.

You see, my friend had been in a very serious accident about three years ago. It took a long time to settle the case. She had gone through a lot of pain and suffering, so many doctors and she had a couple of serious operations. Now my friend had been recuperating from this accident, she had to borrow money to pay rent and to buy food. Her electricity was cut-off and she was behind in her car note. Finally, she had to ask welfare for help. But now everything was good. The money had finally arrived. She wanted me to come right over to help celebrate. I said, "Okay I will be over as soon as my session is over". After the session was over, I left. On the way to my friend's house, I thought about all that she had gone through and I thanked God that now it could be a little easier on her.

I arrived at the house and, to my surprise, I heard loud music and laughing and talking coming from the apartment. I knocked, but no one heard me so I opened the door and went on in. There were wall-to-wall people in the apartment. There was plenty of food and drinks. I was looking from room-to-room for my friend. I didn't know anyone who was at the house. So I spoke to different people there — asking them where my friend was. They were so "high", they just laughed at me and kept on doing what they were doing. The music was so loud I was surprised that no one had called the police. Finally I saw my friend unconscious on the floor. Someone said she would be okay — to give her about 15 minutes — she would come around. I looked at my friend.

She looked so still. I kept calling and calling her name — trying to revive her. When I looked around the room again, I saw so much crack cocaine — more crack than I had ever seen before. I felt so sad. I kneeled down and put my friend's head in my lap. I tried patting and putting water on her face, calling her name over and over.

When my friend didn't respond, I panicked and screamed out, "Turn off that music!" No one paid me any attention. So I jumped up, ran over, turned off the music and called 911. I started to cry and pray. The people there were complaining because the music was cut off. By now they knew something was wrong. They found out that the police were coming. Some of them took the drugs and anything else they could get their hands on and they got out of there. The rest of them were so "stoned", they didn't know what was going on. They just stayed where they were.

Finally, when the paramedics arrived, they immediately started asking questions about what had happened. I tried to explain, but I didn't know all of the answers. I told them that when I arrived my friend was on the floor unconscious. The police wanted to know why it had taken so long to call for help. They called in for backup and took the people who were there into the police station. The police were looking around and they knew exactly what had been going on. The paramedics worked so hard trying to revive my friend, but it was too late. She was dead. Her heart just couldn't take it anymore.

The police asked if I knew the family. I gave them the information that they needed and followed them to the parents' house. They were such nice people. They always tried to instill good values in their children. My friend never wanted her parents to find out about the drugs and alcohol problem. She swore it would never happen again. I found out it always did — time after time. I was there with the parents when the police told them what had happened. They couldn't believe it. After all, they had just talked to their child. They knew all about the money and thought everything was okay. They were in shock and kept on saying, "How could this be!" They just couldn't believe it.

The police asked the family to come down to identify the body. They waited for the other children and they all went together. After identifying the body, they just sat around holding each other — trying to make some kind of sense out of this. The family thought about the bad accident that their child was in. They also reflected that although she might have died from the experience, God brought her through. And it continued as someone expressed, "Oh, the pain and suffering this family is going through!" The mother, all in tears, said that when other people get a large sum of money they pay off their bills. Then they go shopping, buying all the things that they couldn't afford until the money came. She cried out, "They don't end up dead, they don't end up dead!?" I didn't say anything to her, but her child was hooked on drugs and that was the only thing that you think about when you are hooked. You don't care about family or anything else except getting enough money to buy more drugs. Those on drugs spend every dollar they get, even their food stamps, and will "hock" or sell their furniture. They will spend EVERYTHING to buy drugs.

I stayed with the family for a long while trying to show my sympathy to the family. I left and started for home, but my mind kept going back to this family and all the pain and suffering they were going through. I started to wonder, "How could you put your family through all of this pain? Once you overdose, you are dead. Your life stops. It is over. Since the person who was on the drugs is gone, they never know what they put their families through. What if, after you are dead, you could see and hear what is going on, but you can't say anything? First, you would see all of your friends all around you eating and drinking everything in sight — trying to stay long enough to use all of your crack and steal everything they can get their hands on. Before the police come, you are screaming for them to help you.

You would then see yourself running from friend to friend begging them to help you. But they don't have time to respond to you because they are trying to get all that they can get before the police come. Now you realize just what kind of friends you have. If they were your friends, when you first passed out, they would have called 911. If they did, it might have saved your life. The next thing you see and hear is the paramedics working so desperately to do all they can do — trying to save your life, but it is too late.

The police are going through your house looking for answers — trying to find out what happened to you. Now it is time for the police to tell your parents about your death. I can just see you pleading with the police not to tell your parents about your drug habit. By this time, the police are knocking on the door. Your father answered it. The police tell your father all that they know. Your father is in shock as he listens to the policeman talk. He is interrupted by your mother coming into the room. She is hysterical, asking your father what is going on. What's wrong! Your father is crying and shaking so nervously — and is trying to tell your mother that you are dead.

The policeman tells your mother what happened to you. She passes out and the policeman calls the paramedics to revive her. These might have been the same ones who worked on you. How could you do them this way? But you never thought about them did you? You just thought about that drug, nothing else. Look at them! Look into their faces! Look at the pain that they are in! A neighbor came in to help. She calls all of your sisters and your brother. They immediately came over. Now the whole family is in such a turmoil. Who would ever think that one person could cause all of this grief? All of this heartache! Everyone is trying to comfort one another. After the family has calmed down some, the policeman asks them to go down and identify your body. You thought telling them about your death was hard?

What now! How can they take any more? As they look at you, you are so still. You look so sweet and innocent.

As you look on, you try to talk to them. You try to comfort them, but they can't hear you. They will never hear your voice again. Now you would think that their problems are over. No! They have just begun. Your brother angrily asks your friends who got you started on drugs. How long have you been on "the stuff"? But he is blaming the wrong one, isn't he? We always want to blame someone else for our loved one's downfall. But no one is to blame. No one made you do it. It was YOUR decision. Well, friend, just sit back and watch. I don't want you to miss a thing. Now it is time for them to pick out your casket and your final outfit for burial. How sad. They should be picking out a graduation outfit and watching you try on your cap and gown — or even your wedding apparel. They will never see you in anything like that because you decided that you could beat the odds.

Now comes the big day. Not your graduation day or your wedding. No! It is your funeral. The funeral car pulls up with all of your family in it. Look at them! Look into their faces! Do you think that they will ever be happy again? Now they walk up to view your body. They have you so beautifully dressed. You look like a little princess. As they look upon your body they think about the day that you were born. It was not so many years ago that your father held his precious little baby in his arms. As your father and mother sat in that hospital room, they were so happy. You were just what they wanted. You were perfect. All of your life they nurtured and watched you grow. They thought you had your whole life ahead of you.

Now they are standing at your casket looking into the face of this precious child that they brought into the world. The church begins to fill up now. A lot of your friends from school have come, and also your drug buddies are here. Some of them look so young you would think that they had their whole lives ahead of them. They are slowly killing themselves As you watch your friends coming into the church for the first time, you can see what kind of shape your friends are in. When you were "getting high" with them you couldn't see how bad they looked but, now, as you look at them it makes you cry. You are pleading with them to stop before it is too late. You are now screaming at them, "Look at me, look what happened to me! It killed me! The drugs killed me! Don't let this happen to you! Please take a look at my family! Look how they are suffering! Don't let what happened to my family happen to yours!"

We all knew what was in the drugs every time we used them. But we still bought the drugs. Every time we use drugs, we are jeopardizing our lives. As you look around, you see your drug dealer. He also came to view your body. He sent a big bouquet of flowers. After all, you were a very good customer of his. There he sits wearing his fancy suit and his diamonds flashing. He is scanning the room looking for other victims. After all, business is business to him. At the service, the program is planned just right. The singing is so spiritual, and a few of your friends spoke about the good things they remembered about you. Then it was time for your eulogy. A young preacher steps up to the pulpit. He offers a very moving prayer. Then he looks around the room at your grieving family and at all of the young people there. So young in age but looking like they are much older than they should look. They are slowly, slowly killing themselves. He asked the Holy Spirit to help him turn these young people around. He told them about the love of Jesus Christ — how He loved them and wanted them to turn their lives around. And how drugs are just part-time, but Jesus is real and forever.

There are so many tears, so much sorrow and so many young people with no future. They are just doing anything to support their habit as they sit there wondering what could have happened. They are thinking, "We were having such a good time at the party. Who would have ever thought it would end like this?" Now your service is over. Your family is led out behind your casket. That's right. It's not over for your family yet! Now you are driven in a hearse. Your family is right behind you on the way to the cemetery. Finally you arrive at your final resting place. After the preacher says his last words, you are slowly lowered into the ground — gone forever until Jesus comes again. You are at peace, but what about your family. They will never forget the way that you died. Their lives will never be the same.

It is too late for my friend and my friend's family. We all know that when a person dies, they know nothing. They cannot see nor hear anything. At the time of death their life ceases. But their families are still here missing them and trying to go on with their lives. And they will never forget all that they have gone through since your death. But to anyone who thinks that drugs "are the way to go in the 90's", don't be misled. The next time you put a pipe to your mouth, a needle in your vein or even inhale spray paint trying to get that "great high", you are playing Russian Roulette with your lives. The only difference is you play Russian Roulette with a gun, but you are playing it with a pipe, or needle or sandwich bags. If you keep on, you will hit the jackpot. Your heart will just stop.

What kind of future will you young people have? Do you think about a future? Young girls are pregnant, babies are born on crack and never have a chance. Other children born in the world are either physically or sexually abused by their own parents. How can they mistreat their own children that way? And then there is aids. They are killing our young people left and right. Young people are killing each other on the street. Our school children are carrying guns and knives to school. They are going to jail as adults because they commit such serious crimes. There used to be a time when you would be attending a senior citizen's funeral but, now, our seniors are living a long, productive life. And we are burying our children each and every day. Our children need God's help.

They think they know everything and they don't know anything. They think they have everything. But what do they really have? Nothing but trouble!

Each and every day our young people are getting themselves deeper and deeper in trouble. When will they stop? Do they have to go to jail or almost die before they admit that they need our help? GOD HAVE MERCY ON OUR CHILDREN AND YOUNG PEOPLE! They are running to and from place to place LOOKING FOR LOVE, PEACE AND HAPPINESS! The only thing they find is sorrow. Young people, you are looking in the wrong place. DROP DOWN ON YOUR KNEES YOUNG PEOPLE! TALK TO YOUR HEAVENLY FATHER! HE HAS PROMISED TO LISTEN! FIND COMFORT IN **HIS** HOLY WORD.

WHERE THERE IS GOD — THERE IS NO NEED!

Standing in Line

Each week on the Sabbath the Bright and Morning Star Ministry Team meets to feed the homeless who come to the park and, also, the elderly who never receive enough money for food. The people in the drop-in center can't go home and cook a meal. They don't have a place to call home and that's why we want to, at least once a week on God's Sabbath day, give the people a very good meal. We know that the people in the neighborhood have found out about the good meals that are being served week after week, so when they see us coming they come running with children in hand and in strollers to get the free meal that is being served in the park. You can hear them telling their children, "You better eat because I'm not going to cook today". If you don't have a meal then you are welcome to come and eat with us, but you are missing the whole purpose of our mission. It is not our goal to see how full you can get. It is not our goal to try and outdo any other group. We are not even trying to make sure that we have the largest crowd. We are here to do what Jesus would want us to do. He told us to feed His people, teach them about His love. And that, my friends, is our mission down there in the park — to do the will of our Lord Jesus Christ.

Jesus will tell us in that day, "I was hungry and ye gave me meat, thirsty and ye gave me drink". Then the righteous will ask Jesus, "When did we see you hungry and gave you food, thirsty and gave you drink?" And the King will answer and say unto them, "Verily I say unto you inasmuch as ye have done it unto one of the least of these my brethren ye have done it unto me" (Matt. 25:35-40). This is what this whole team wants Jesus to say to us one day. No one in this group is rich. No one has money or food just handed to us. What you see here are hardworking people working each and every week to fill these pots and, believe me, it takes a lot of money and time. Remember one thing, no one has to come and do this for you. We are not getting paid to feed you. We do it because we love you and we all love the Lord. We need the Lord. We need the Lord in everything that we do and He has promised to be there for us and take care of us.

But when you are standing in line waiting to be fed and the team starts to sing and to testify praising the Lord, no one wants to leave their place in line to praise the Lord. So you don't move from the line and, after you eat, you leave so you don't even hear the sermon that the pastor has prepared for you from the Lord. So, you just come in the park for the free meal. Some of you have a lot of complaints. Why? You didn't pay for the meal. What do you have to complain about? Listen people, we are there to serve the Lord. Always give Him the praise in song, in scripture and, always, in prayer. We want God's blessing. We know without Him we could not fill up these pots week after week. We cook like we are feeding the Lord each week because how can we say we love the Lord who we have not seen and treat our brothers and sisters any kind of way.

The way we treat people and the quality in the food we prepare always is the best we can do.

And always keep in mind that Saturday is the Sabbath day. God Himself blessed the seventh day and sanctified it. Jesus said, where two or more are gathered together in His name there He is in the midst of us. So we come together each and every week knowing that Christ is there with us. Read your Bible every day. Pray to God every day and, when you come to the park on the Sabbath, always remember that the Lord is always there with us. Some people ask, "Where is your church"? The church is within your heart. Although we are not always inside of a building you can still find the Lord. He's in the midst of us. Wherever you are look for Him, seek Him, learn all that the Lord has in store for you.

**WHERE FOOD IS SOON DIGESTED AND GONE,
THE WORD OF GOD LASTS FOREVER!**

Wonder If?

People need so much in life, even though they are grown. They almost have to be spoon-fed like a baby by God. Just stop and think about this for a moment. People may say that they love God and that they would do anything for Him, but most of them will only do for God when it is most convenient for them. They can't sacrifice anything or any time for the Lord's work. They make all kinds of excuses to keep from obeying Him. They are too young or living for Christ is too hard. Are you too young? Christ was only thirty-three years old when He died for our sins. Wonder if Jesus was like us? Wonder if Jesus became too tired to take care of us? We need Jesus 24 hours a day. We could never go without His help. "Never!" We all know that Jesus owns everything in this world. Wonder if He decided to keep everything for Himself and not give us anything? How would we feel about Him? Wonder if Jesus would treat us the way we treat Him?

Let's say for instance Jesus would ask you to witness to the less fortunate and you tell Him, "I will, but not now!" Then He could respond with, "Okay then I will not send the sun to shine on you today". Or say you don't feel like going to church today because you are too tired or too busy. Then Jesus would just refuse to wake you up in the morning. And if you figure that God doesn't need your tithes, then Jesus wouldn't see any need of taking care of your family. Why would He waste His time taking care of us when we don't care about Him? And the way we stand up and curse God, as loving and caring as God is, how can we "do" God the way that we do? And the way we act when we are asked to do a job for Him. We carry on as though we could care less. Wonder if the Lord did us the same? If Jesus would say, "I'm tired of taking care of them?" Or wonder if He would tell His Father, "let someone else take care of them. I'm all burned out! I have always taken care of them. I have done it long enough." What would happen to us? How would we live? How could we survive without Christ.

Have you ever stopped to think about Christ and His love — the way we ruin our lives with drinking, smoking, taking drugs, doing whatever Satan wants us to do. Jesus should step aside and let us have our way since that's what we seem to want. When Satan gets finished knocking and beating us around, we will be begging for Jesus to come back into our lives. But Jesus is not like that. He loves us so much that He came down here and died for us all. His nail print hands and feet prove that He loves us more than anyone could ever love mankind.

He gives us so many chances day by day. We can always count on Him day or night. If Jesus would ask us to do something, the first thing we do is to make excuses. But would you be too tired or would you have the time if the church would offer to pay you for your services? Why do we have to be paid for doing God's work? Did we pay Jesus when He died for us.? How much did he charge? Wonder if He charged us for each drive He took as the nails were driven into His hands and feet? And how much should He charge us for the insults He had to take? And how much should we pay Jesus for the bruises and for the spitting in His face. Jesus had to take all of this from the people. How much should He charge us? How much? Would we be willing to take the pain that Jesus had to bear for us? Then there were the thorns from the crown that they put upon His head. And He never said a word. Wonder if Jesus charged us for every minute, hour, and day you breathe God's breath on this earth? Wonder if God would do us the way we do Him?

What Would Happen If Jesus Would Come Today?

I stay up late at night and sometimes I start to wonder about Jesus and the end of the world. I was talking to a sister of mine and I was telling her how I overcame a lot of problems. I told her when I had a challenge in my life, I would talk to Jesus first. Then I would say to myself, "I wonder if while I was in the act of sin, what would happen if that was the time that Jesus would come in the clouds back to this earth" (what if this is the day that Jesus comes back to this earth). One day in late summer, as I was doing my daily routine, I was waiting for my ride because we were all going out that evening. This was my night to go out with my friends. I had to look my best, carry the right purse, and wear the right shoes to match my dress. But, in the back of my mind, I had thought about going to visit my church. I was brought up in the church. My parents took me all the time. As I got ready to go out I was thinking, "But God knows my heart! He is aware that I really love Him, and when I get finished running around and quit doing what I am doing now I will get back in church. I bet I will be a good Christian too. But, right now, I have too much going for me to think about church.

For now, I just have to put all these thoughts out of my mind. But I continued to ponder:

"I wonder what Clare will have on? She always tries to outdo everyone else. Oh I hope Henry drives his brand new sports car. Oh boy, would I look good in that. If God would see fit to give me a brand new car I would go to church all the time. I would show the good old church people just how well I am getting along. Well I'm not doing so bad. I have a lot of things that I need — a nice house, pretty clothes, and a little money. Well, let me finish dressing because they will be here soon."

But, for some reason, my mind just kept going back to Jesus.

"I pray at night. I say my blessings before I eat. I know I don't go to church, but I'm not doing a lot of bad things in my life. Oh why? Why am I thinking about Jesus again? Okay, I am going to put this out of my mind and get ready. Here comes my friends. I hope I don't think about this again. It is so depressing."

As we stopped at the light I heard singing coming from the church, and it was the church I used to attend as a child. It was the middle of the week and I wondered what the church was doing open. I found out that it was choir rehearsal. I could hear them singing as we waited at the light. And I remembered that I used to sing in the choir. That brought back the same thoughts I had at the house. I felt so uncomfortable now — more than ever But, after a while, I soon shook off those feelings because we had arrived at our favorite place and I heard another type of music coming from inside. I thought to myself,

"This is better! Let's party!" I put everything in the back of my mind and started to have fun with my friends. We were having a ball. Nothing mattered now. No, nothing at all. You see as I look back on my life, I reflect on how I was brought up in the church, baptized as a child and again as an adult. Even kept the Sabbath from sunset to sunset. I thought I was "in good" with the Lord. I thought God would understand that I was weak and that I really did love Him. So I went on with my life as though I would live forever — as though I would never die. I was young. I had my life all ahead of me. I just knew I had years to get my life in order.

You know how it is. You think, "When I get older I will settle down and then I will give my all to Jesus. I'm just not ready now — too much living to do, places to go. I am looking for a very rich and handsome man in my life, so many dreams to fill." Well, back to my story. We were really having a good time, good food, drinks and smokes. Yes, we had it all. Then, all of a sudden, there was a loud noise like thunder. It hit again and again. The music stopped and everyone ran to look outside. I saw people running wild in the street. I looked up and I was stunned. Oh, the bright lights that were in the sky! It got brighter and brighter — larger and larger until the clouds were opening up and it looked like a figure of a man! At first I thought it was a tornado. As I ran like the others I kept looking up and, by now, the figure was getting closer and closer. It looked like lots and lots of angels with Him at this time. I was scared! I just wanted to hide from this scene. I was saying, "I couldn't believe my eyes!" The people were crying, pleading and begging for their lives. I kept saying, "Not now, not today! I'm not ready, not ready! I thought I had more time, a lot more time! Jesus can't be coming today!" I had no idea why I had been thinking about Jesus today. Now I do! I had been so uncomfortable all day. "Oh, why! Why didn't I listen! Instead of trying to get my soul right with Christ I was busy trying to get out in the streets. Oh how I wish things could be different. Oh how I wish I had another chance to live my life over!?

The Holy Spirit was trying to warn me but I was too dumb to listen. Now it's too late. Too late for me to ask forgiveness for my sins. Now the noise got louder and louder, and I remembered what the preacher said in one of his sermons. "As it was in the days of Noah there was eating and drinking, marrying and giving in marriage. So shall it be in the day when the son of Man comes. And Jesus will say, "if you are righteous let them be righteous still. And if you be just let them be just still. and if you be filthy let them be filthy still." Oh my God I don't have a chance to change. I am doomed. I am doomed. All of my life I have heard that Jesus is coming. But who believed it would be today. Not today! At this point I kept saying over and over — "Not today!" Then I looked up one more time. Jesus and His angels are getting closer and closer. And I could feel the trembling and opening up of the earth, and people were coming up and meeting the Lord. Some people were looking up and waiting for the Lord.

Cars and people were running into each other. Money and jewelry were all in the street. People were running into the streets. Now it doesn't matter if I have the right clothes and the right shoes and purse, I wish I had Jesus in my heart. I wish I had built my treasure in heaven. "Oh how I wish I only had a minute to ask God to forgive me. But I know He gave me a whole lifetime. I just did not heed His warning.

'OH MY GOD I AM LOST, I AM LOST..."

Let Your Conscience Be Your Guide

Things happen to us during the course of a week. Sometimes we have to make sudden decisions and, from time-to-time, they might not be the ones that Christ would make. Later on, we might wonder, "Did I do the right thing?" Well, we don't have to ask anyone. Our conscience will let us know. If we make the wrong choice, our conscience will just bother us every minute of the day. Sometimes we might ask another person, "Do you think I made the right decision?" We try to tell the other person all the right facts to make the person come to the same conclusion that we have come to. But, in our heart, we knew that it was not right and our conscience will bother us day and night until we make that thing right. And I thank God for my conscience, because it makes me honest. But whatever we do during the week, on Sabbath when we come to church, we are so clean, wholesome and so sanctified. We look as thought we should be sitting right next to Christ Himself — looking just like we should be sprouting wings and wearing our long white robes. We sing and shout and pray for a long period of time asking God for the same thing over and over again.

We go into other people's home pretending to care for them — and trying to gain their confidence. And, at the same time, we try to find out all of their "business" and downfalls. Then, when you find out all that you need to know, we "turn" on that person. The next thing you know, all of their business is all over the church. But no one knows what we have been doing during the week. Day after day, week after week our little secret is safe so we think. Others look at us and they want to be like us. We look and act just like the perfect Christian. In the dark, some love to use drugs. But, because they don't do it all of the time, everything is alright because no ones knows.

Some of us love to drink. We feel like a little beer or wine won't hurt. After all, we are not drinking all of the time. And the ones who have a "shot" of liquor each evening might say, "I need a drink at night to unwind after a hard day at work. What could it hurt?" Some might love to smoke. Well, what would be wrong with a cigarette, pipe or maybe a cigar? No one can see you! There is no one here but you. Some of us might love to "play around" with some of the dear brothers or sisters in the church or neighborhood. We feel as long as we keep it a secret, no one would ever know.

But, dear saints, Jesus knows all! Because you feel that your sins are not as bad as what the other person is guilty of, you feel that you have the right to help straighten out someone else's life. And what is worse we sometimes, as Christians, start to believe we have done what is right when we bring someone's else's mistakes to "light". God wants us to be true Christians. He wants us to truly love Him with all of our hearts. Make your life an open book to Jesus. Clean up your life! If you have anything in your life, you know whether or not

Jesus is pleased with you. Let your conscience be your guide. No one may ever know what you do when you are alone. You might think that you have gotten away with sin in your life. Remember God knows all, and is writing every unkind deed that we do and every unkind word that we speak. And, if we don't change our life, one day God will uncover all of our sins. What we do in the dark will come out in the light. If every week there was a sign across our chest showing sins that we have committed during the week, we wouldn't be so quick to point out someone else's shortcomings.

We all want to strive to be the best Christians we can be. We are in the last days brothers and sisters. If you claim to be a Christian, you have already given up so many things that you thought were fun, but really only got you into trouble. Time is so short. We don't have time to be phony. The time we take practicing to be a fake Christian, we could be putting that time into studying the word of God. In God's word He tells us how to be the best Christians in the world. Follow His word! When we pray, ask Jesus to lay our life out before Him as an open book so if there is anything in our lives that needs to be cleaned up, Jesus is there to clean us up. In life, do we want praise from men or women? Do we need them to tell us what a good Christian we are? If that's what we want, then we have our reward right here on earth. But, if we want God's love, we have to be true to God. He knows our every move before we do it. We could never fool the Lord. If you are faithful to Jesus, one day He will be waiting for you with open arms to take you home with Him to Heaven to live in the beautiful mansions that He has prepared for you.

LET YOUR CONSCIENCE BE YOUR GUIDE!

Stand Up and Choose You This Day
Who You Will Serve

You have so many decisions to make in your young life. Today's young people look so sad. They shouldn't have a care in the world. They seem to carry the burdens of the world on their shoulders. Our young people worry about things that they shouldn't think about for years to come. You would think because they are young that they would be carefree and fancy-free but, instead, they are so unhappy. One thing everyone is looking for and needs is LOVE. While looking for that small four-letter word, most young people will do anything. That's how they get involved in drugs, gangs, or even sex trying to find love.

Some of our young people feel that they don't have to work for people of other races. But who do they think they are working for when they are selling drugs? they are selling the drugs to our children, young adults and pregnant women. It is a quick way to make a buck but, in the end, do our young people think that it is worth it? Not only do our young people sell drugs, they even take any kinds of drugs. They don't care what is in them. They just want to feel good. When they hear on television that a drug is bad and people are getting sick or dying from it, the young people run to find that particular drug. They want to find out what will happen to THEM if they take this drug. They seem to love to take chances with their lives. Young people — STAND UP AND CHOOSE YOU THIS DAY WHO YOU WILL SERVE! When you choose Christ, you don't need to have drugs in your body to make you feel good. You won't have to have multiple sex partners to fill your needs. You don't have to sell drugs to make your money. All you need to do is to choose who you will serve — Christ or Satan.

Christ will take all of those cravings for drugs or sex from your body. He will give you a clean body. He will open doors for you in order for you to make a good living. Just trust Him with all your heart. The gang leaders tell you that they love you in order to get your trust. They have signs and you will obey them without asking any questions. They are not your friends. They are only using you. When you get into trouble the gangs are gone and you are left alone, because they are from Satan and we know that he doesn't care. Sometimes young people are forced to carry a gun to make them look like a "real" man or woman. Remember once you pull that trigger, you become a man or woman regardless of how old you are. In gangs you have to prove that you are willing to obey the gang leaders by beating other young people up. This makes you a "big" man or woman. But, sometimes, the tables "turn" and you get beat up or shot. When you pull that trigger and shoot someone or when someone pulls the trigger and shoots you, either way your life is over. Stop and think young person. Is this all your life is about.

Young people before you put that gun in your hand, before you obey that gang leader's commands that he gives you, STOP - STAND UP AND CHOOSE YOU THIS DAY WHO YOU WILL SERVE. Do this not with a gun in your hand, not with your fist ready to fight, but with the word of God in your hand and a prayer on your lips. Young ladies, I know that you are looking for love from that special young man. But every time a young man says those beautiful words (I LOVE YOU), it doesn't necessarily mean that he is telling you the truth. Sometimes that young man knows that's what you want to hear so that's what he will tell you — and many more young ladies.

When he gets what he wants, he might leave you for someone else. Maybe now, you have a baby on the way. Oh, how alone you feel and that young man has moved on to the next young lady — leaving you pregnant and with no future.

Young lady, before you give in to that young man, STAND UP AND TELL HIM, "I am well loved by Jesus Christ. He loves me with an unconditional love. I will never be alone as long as I have the love of my Heavenly Father. I don't need artificial love. I HAVE THE REAL THING!"

Why Worry? Why Fret?

Each and every day of our lives we, as human beings, worry. We agonize about things that we can't do anything about. I think that if Americans didn't have anything to worry about they wouldn't make it. We say that we believe in God, and we trust Him with all of our hearts. We get up in church and testify about how we have taken our problems to the Lord and how He has worked them out for us. We cry and shout the praises to God. People around us might say how great we are. But, we must really learn to trust the Lord. You go home and you once again start worrying about your problems. We testify that we have laid our problems at the altar and we will let God work it out for us. But we find ourselves worrying about our problems again. We get sick, our hair starts coming out, we start losing weight, and no one knows why. Maybe when you turned your problems over to the Lord, and He didn't work fast enough for you so you picked your problem back up.

I'm just wondering if your worrying about your problems solved anything. As bad as you look, all of your problems should be over. But they are not. They are worse. Maybe your faith was strong at one time. Possibly you really believe that God could help you. Maybe you lost your home that you had for years. Maybe your furniture and car are gone. It is so hard when your children are on drugs or in jail, and there is no way for you to help them. So you sit and worry, day and night, until you end up in the hospital on all kinds of pills. But, believe it or not, after all of that you still have the same problems — only now they are worse. You see, the Lord knows when we are sincere because He can see right through us.

When you come before the lord, be for real! Don't try to fool Him! Your prayers will fall on deaf ears. That's when we feel that God is not listening to our prayers. When we are not sincere, God knows! Just because you can pray long prayers and testify so that everyone is in tears doesn't make you alright with God. Sometimes you look around and a person might not know how to pray like you do. Maybe all that they know is, "Lord have mercy on me," and it seems that God answers their prayers. But you don't understand why God is not answering your prayers. After all, you know how to pray long prayers.

Your testimony is so moving that it can bring tears to your eyes. But it doesn't seem that God answered your prayers any faster. You wonder why God doesn't answer your prayers. After all, you know how to pray. You know how to testify, and you pray whenever someone needs you to pray. So you think that you have a line straight up to Heaven. But God is not answering your prayers. As you look around, you see your neighbors are doing fine. They have nice homes and cars. It even seems that they have money. They don't have a care in the world. But you seem to always be worrying about something. You never seem to be at peace. It seems that God is not listening to you. You wonder why He doesn't care about you. God doesn't move on OUR time. He moves RIGHT ON TIME, according to HIS TIMETABLE.

God has to teach you patience. Always remember that God listens to us. He loves us and He is there to help us with our problems. All we have to do is to have faith in Him. Trust Him with all our heart and soul. You don't have to pray long drawn-out prayers for God to listen to you. He is not impressed with your long prayers. Man might be, but God isn't. He knows you. He knows just what you are made of. As for those long prayers, the only thing you get is sore knees and the people listening to you are wishing that you would hurry up and finish that long drawn-out prayer. You think that everyone is impressed with your prayer, but they are not. If you would look around while you are praying, you would see how bored people really are. When you go home after a long Prayer Service, you don't put into practice what you have been praying about. You start back worrying about your problems again.

When you wake up and open your eyes, the first thing you should do is to thank the good Lord for waking you up and keeping you in your right mind. But, sometimes, we forget about how good God is to us. We forget about how good God has been to our families, and for giving us another day. But instead we start back worrying about where we will live, a car, money, all tyes of material things, our children and what they are doing with their lives. With all of the worrying we do, how do we think that the Holy Spirit can speak to us when our minds are all clogged up with worry? There is no way that we can say that we love the Lord and trust Him, if all that you do is to worry. Christian people, you never have to worry. You never have to fret. God is our co-pilot and, if you will let Him lead you through all walks of life, then you will never worry again. That's the only way that you can have that inner peace in your life.

Worry will give you all kinds of health problems such as high blood pressure, sugar diabetes, headaches and many other illnesses. So, don't worry! Don't fret! When things are not going right in your life, don't throw up your hands and holler, "Oh Lord, why me!" CALL ON JESUS with all of your heart, then get up and leave your burden there. In His word He tells you to trust in Him and your yoke is easy and your burdens are light (Matthew 11:30).

Turn the Other Cheek

One thing we need to learn in this life is to turn the other cheek. That is so hard to do because, when someone does something to you, the only thing you want to do is to "get even" with them. You think about it day and night, wondering how they could have treated you this way. Any time you have a moment alone to maybe rest or try to go to sleep, sometimes the only thing that keeps going through your mind is that person and what they have done to you. Piece by piece you think about what happened and what was said — over and over in your mind until it nearly drives you crazy. You keep pondering, "how could that person do this to me? How could they treat me this way?" You think about how good you were to them, and how things have turned out. Don't give a person so much control over you. Don't let them know that they have taken over your life. You have to learn to put it behind you and get on with your life. You have to! You can't keep thinking and thinking about the same thing over and over again.

Every time that person comes into your mind, ask the Lord to put it behind you and go on with your life. God loves you and He sees and knows everything that goes on in your life, and the angel of the Lord has already written down all of the good deeds that you have done. He will reward you for them. You might think that this person has really done you wrong and, maybe, they seem to have the upper hand. After you have helped them so, you feel you have lost a great deal. But remember, when you have God on your side, He will never let you down. He will stand by you all the way, and you will have more than you have ever had because you have helped someone else. In Matthew 22:37, 38, 39, Jesus said you should love the Lord your God with all your heart, all your soul and all your mind. This is the first and most important commandment. And the next one is just like it. You should love and value your neighbor as much as you love and value yourself (clear word Bible).

So when you do something nice for someone else, you are doing it for God. You have a peaceful mind. He doesn't want you to be worried. There is no need to be so troubled that you can't find your way out. If you really love the Lord as you say that you do, you shouldn't have any problems. If someone treats you badly, turn them over to the Lord. Take them to the altar and leave them there. Satan loves to control your mind and, if your mind is so clogged up with worries, Satan will keep you thinking about everything someone has ever done to you so that you can't hear what the Father has to say to you. Sometimes people use their troubles as an excuse to use drugs or drink alcohol, claiming that they are too depressed to go on. So they are letting the person who has already hurt them once, do it over and over again.

Remember, one day Jesus will come back for us and He will say to those on His right side, "You are God's children. You have cared about others so I know that you care about me. When they were thirsty, you gave them drink. When they were hungry, you gave them food, and when they had no place to stay, you took them in. When they had nothing suitable to wear, you gave them clothes. When they were sick, you visited and comforted them. And when they were in jail, you didn't forget them". The righteous will say, "Lord we never realized that when we fed the hungry we were feeding you. When we gave them a drink, we were giving it to you. When they were sick and in prison, we were standing by you." The Son of God will say, "I know that you didn't realize this because a change took place in your life and kindness and compassion became a part of your nature" (Matt: 25). So, Saints, learn to turn the other cheek, and let the Lord handle all of your troubles.

Wade in the Water

We, as Christians, should have a new name. We need to be called "Surface Christians". The definition of a "Surface Christian" is they love to be in the spotlight praising the Lord in public. In some people's eyes it seems as though they are true Christians, but they are "Surface Christians". A "Surface Christian" loves to dress up in their Sabbath best, sit up in front of church with their ruffles and lace on their silk and satin outfits, matching suits and shoes — just singing and shouting the praising of the Lord. They are always walking around making sure that they are noticed. When we get out of our big expensive cars and go into the church, we walk in with our heads held high. When people pass by us, they don't see Christ through us. The only way the people know that you are going to church is because they see you going through the church doors.

Those who are "Surface Christians" don't mind cooking a dish for a church dinner. They don't even mind serving a meal. They might give away a few clothes to the needy and, when called upon, they will give food to feed the hungry. Afterward they stand up in church to give account of all the clothes and food they have given away. They tell how they went into their closets and pulled out shoes and clothes and how they cleaned out their freezers to feed the poor. Sometimes they even give a little money to help out — and stand up and tell the church everything they have done. They don't leave anything out while someone is writing down everything that is being said. Only God knows if what you are saying is the truth or not.

We all need to get off of our backsides and roll up our sleeves. There is work to be done! It's okay that we meet up at church and have a good service, good singing, good sermons, and a powerful prayer. It's okay to get together and fellowship. That's fine! But, after all, we need to get up off that pew at church and look around. You have the elderly. They are the backbone of our church. They were the pioneers of the church. They not only supported the church but they invested their hard-earned money for over 50 and 60 years — never complaining, only working hard. But now they are older and need our help. They need to know that someone cares. After all they have given all of their lives to their church. Shouldn't their church now give them something back? It seems that they are forgotten.

Let us remember our elderly — go into their homes, cook for them, wash their clothes and clean their homes. Sometimes they just need someone to spend the night with them because they are sick. Sometimes they are afraid to spend the night alone. Be there to give them a bath. Most of them don't have a family anymore. They are all gone now. The church should be their family. After all, you ARE called their church family. There are so many single mothers in our churches and neighborhoods. They need our help! Open your eyes, look around and see our young children with no one but their mothers to count on.

Where are we as a church? I will tell you what happens as a church. You see your neighbor's child getting into trouble or you hear the mother of a young child standing up testifying about how worried she is for her child. And you, as a Christian, just shake your head and say, "I will pray for you and your child". But, sometimes you do and sometimes you forget. Don't be afraid to get your hands dirty! Don't be afraid to reach out to help that parent or young child. That's your job as a child of the King! Get up! Put your arms around that family! Let them know that you're there for them. Let them see Christ in you! TO WADE IN THE WATER SOMETIMES MEANS PUTTING ON YOUR KNEE BOOTS AND GETTING DIRTY.

You might have to stop that drug dealer from selling drugs right in front of the church. You might have to pick up beer bottles in front of the church. You might have to go into the bar to reach that person who needs to know about the Lord. Whatever you have to do, do it because one day Jesus will say to us, "I was hungry and you gave me no meat. I was thirsty and you gave me no drink. I was in prison and you visited me not. And you will look at Jesus and say, "Father I have been in the church singing and shouting your praises all of my life. I have given money, food and clothes to the poor. I couldn't go out in the field Lord because I wouldn't know what to say to the people, but you can look in the record book and see everything that I have accomplished". You might have a smile on your face waiting for the Lord's answer. And the Lord will look at you and say, "DEPART FROM ME I KNOW YOU NOT".

God's Precious Cargo

God one day gathered up His little seeds, and He planted them gently inside each of His carrying cases — which is us. His little bundles are placed very tenderly so that they would be well protected and preserved for the long journey ahead. He made a way so that His little bundles could be fed and they could grow and get stronger and stronger, bigger and bigger until the end of their journey. The only thing that the ones who carry the precious cargo have to do is to eat right, drink enough water and see the doctor so that His little cargo could get larger and larger and be healthy for its long journey. Each day of the journey God makes sure that His little cargo are protected from the knocks and bumps along the way. The first month the little bundle is so small that you can hardly see it but, month after month, the bundle that was so small starts to grow and grow. Its little features start to appear. The heartbeat can now be heard and this little bundle that was so small is now fully developed as God's precious cargo.

Finally, the bundle reaches its final destination and its journey is all over. What a long haul it has been. Now it is time for the bundle to start down the birth canal. At the end, they face the world for the first time. God is so proud of His little bundle of joy that He gives out a receipt, and you must promise that you will love them. You must cherish them and protect His precious little cargo. After all, this is just a loan from God. When this little bundle is placed into your arms and you open the blanket, you can see why God was so particular about His little cargo. It is a beautiful and wonderful little baby. You can't help smiling when you hold this tiny sweet infant in your arms. You just thank God over and over for the gift. You have to feed the baby — as well as change, bathe and dress it. Sometimes you have to get up late with the baby at night. Other times the baby is sick and cries all the time. But, when you accepted the gift, all of this went along with the gift.

This precious bundle is the most mysterious gift every given to the human race. How they are conceived, then formed in the womb, and finally come down the birth canal and enter into the world is still beyond our understanding. The way the world seems to hate one another, you can't help smiling when you see a sweet little baby. But not everyone seems to see this miracle in the same way. God has blessed us with this wonderful miracle — His little magnificent bundle of joy. How do we treat God's gift to us? Sometimes the carrier of God's precious cargo knows that she is carrying something very special for God, but forgets about God and His precious cargo. The only thing she thinks about is herself and where to find her next "fix". For the nine months that they have ahead of them, the only thing that she thinks about is her drugs and how she is going to get her hands on them. She doesn't eat right or visit the doctor. The only one that she visits is the dope dealer. So God's precious cargo is neglected.

Some make it throughout the long journey. Some are dead along the way. Oh what a waste of God's precious cargo. Sometimes God's gift is treated as if they were trash. Have you ever stopped to think about what is thrown into the trash? Every nasty and smelly thing that you could imagine goes into the trash. Even though people know what goes into the trash, they take a garbage bag and put God's gift into it and throw it away. Sometimes they don't even take time to put it into a bag, they just throw it out of a window. How could you look into the face of that precious cargo and throw it into the trash? Sometimes this little one makes it. Someone finds it before it it too late.

Some just open the window and toss the baby out of the it — like a ball. They don't even care where the child ends up — maybe on top of someone's car or they just crash to the cold ground.

Sometimes they are neglected — they are left alone, not fed, or changed all day and left to starve to death. Some are beaten so badly their bones are broken and become children living in fear. Some children are used by the parents for sexual favors, raping the children over and over. One day you will feel the emptiness in your heart where once a beautiful sweet baby filled your life. Now you have nothing. Children are the most precious thing in the world. God gave His cargo to us to love.

Let us compare God's cargo to your special trip. Let's say you have planned to take this trip for months. Everything is to be so perfect. Not only do you buy a lot of nice clothes, you buy beautiful luggage. Now it is time for your trip, so you take your luggage to the proper place and you leave it. In return, they give you a receipt. With this receipt, they promise to take care of your luggage. At the end of your trip, you take the receipt to the proper place and they give you back your luggage. Now, when you pick up your luggage, you look it over. How will you feel if your luggage is all scarred up or your zipper is broken or maybe it is lost? You become very angry. You will march right over to the desk and demand that they fix your luggage and, if they can't fix it, they will buy you another one. A piece of luggage is just a material thing! It is not flesh and blood! It has no heart, no soul! You can find it on sale!

When God gave us His cargo to love and protect, they are flesh and blood. They have a heart and a soul! They are human beings who are helpless. They need to be taken care of. They need to be loved. Just like God is loved, we need to learn to love. If you know how to love, there can be NO WAY that you can be so heartless as to destroy one of His little ones. God loves His littlest ones so much that He becomes very upset with us as adults because of the way that we care for His little cargo that He was so particular with. You were given God's little bundle of joy to love and protect, to teach them about the Lord and tell them how much the Lord loves them and cherishes them. One day the Lord will be standing there waiting for His little bundles to be given back to Him. When the Lord reaches out His hand to give you His receipt for His little bundles of joy, what are you going to tell Him when He asks you, "Did you take good care of my little cargo?'

How will you answer him? How can you explain the way you discarded:

GOD'S PRECIOUS LITTLE CARGO

Be Not Deceived

I was looking at t.v. one night and it flashed across the screen that the Virgin Mary was coming to this small town in Kentucky. The people started making plans for that miracle. Finally, everything was ready. People came from everywhere to see Mary, who was the earthly mother of Jesus, because she was chosen by God to be His mother. It did not make her holy. She died and is in the grave waiting for Jesus to come back to redeem her and take her to Heaven just like the rest of us. All evening, buttons on cameras were pushed. One after another, people were looking up in the sky — looking at their pictures of the clouds and trying to find a miracle. Oh how easy it is for us to be deceived. Everyone is looking for a miracle in their lives and everyone is looking forward to having something wonderful happen in their lives. Jesus has promised us that if we believe in Him and trust Him that He would cause miracle after miracle to happen in our lives. But that is too simple. Jesus told us to seek Him in prayer and by studying His word. He is all around us watching and waiting for us to come to Him. All we have to do is to ASK.

We don't have to spend a lot of money trying to find a miracle. We don't have to run from city to city looking for that inner peace and always getting disappointed. Jesus has promised us that He will always be there for us when Satan tricks us into believing that we saw something that we didn't even see. But we make ourselves really believe that what we saw was a miracle. What could Mary or any other person who is already dead or will soon get sick and die promise you? Would they have a place to take you to? Why would you look for a dead person? Remember what it says in Ecclesiastes 9:5: "For the living know that they should die but the dead knows not anything". Matt. 7:15 tell us, "Beware of false prophets which come to you in sheep's clothing". If you want to see a miracle in your life, CALL ON JESUS! If you need love, CALL ON JESUS! He is always there.

One day Jesus died for our sins but, THANK GOD, He did something that all of your idols put together could never do. He arose from the dead to save you and me. Don't be deceived! Trust the true Savior! When you truly get to know Him, you won't need that false miracle. KEEP YOUR EYES ON JESUS because with Jesus you have all that you need. Matt. 7:7-8 says, "Ask and it shall be given you, seek and ye shall find, knock and it shall be opened unto you".

The Great Reunion

The family decided that it was time for the big family reunion so they started rushing around calling one another making plans for electing different committees to find the perfect hall that was big enough for the whole family. Another committee was set up to select the right band. Still another committee was created to find the best price on the food. Yet another committee was formed to set a price and collect the money from each family member. And we had to pick a picnic site just perfect for all of the chidren's needs in the family. When the committees met together to compare notes and set a date for the reunion, each head of a committee told all what they had accomplished. Now the great reunion was in motion. Each day the plans seemed to become more and more heckled. No one seemed to agree on anything. No one wanted to take over but they never agreed with the ones that went out of their way to try to make the plans to make this reunion a huge success. Day by day, week by week, the plans went on — sometimes working up into the night. Of course we had to shop for that perfect outfit for that perfect night. That takes weeks of shopping to find that special outfit with all of the accessories to match.

Now it was time to find out if all of the committees had finalized their plans and you find out that some have and some haven't. The worse committee is the Financial Committee, trying to collect the money from each member. So some of the other members volunteered to help collect the money by the due date. There was calling, visiting, and just praying that everything would work out just right when all of a sudden you hear from the Food Committee that the price will be different from what was first quoted. Oh how disappointing this was. We now have to find another hall with someone else to cater the affair or pay the extra price for the hall that we have. So a couple of us went to talk to the owner of the hall that we had rented first. We knew that we couldn't get any more money from the family. After all, we were having trouble collecting the money that was quoted at first. After talking to the owner and making a few adjustments, everything was back on. We now had the hall and the food and, believe it or not, the money was collected. After putting the program into motion it was getting closer to the day. We wondered, "is everything set? Have we missed anything?"

We had one more meeting of the committees to make sure that everything was just right. I don't think that I have ever worried so much in my life. We were waiting for the family who lived out of town to tell us when they would be coming in town so that we could find out how many were coming and we had to find out where they would be staying. The letters and money started coming in. Calls started coming in telling us how many members each family could put up and how long they would be here. There were some members I had never met until now that we were planning this reunion, and they lived right here in the city. So many children. God has really been good to this family. Well the day finally arrived and the night that would be the night of our family reunion banquet. We were so busy running around getting ready for this big night. So much money was spent for this one night trying to look our best. A bunch of us decided to rent a limousine for our big night. As the limo pulled up and we started coming out of the house, everyone looked so nice and we were having such a nice time. It seemed that everything was going to be just right.

When we arrived we could hear the music playing and all of the family started coming. Some on time, some late, some very late. Everyone was so glad to see one another. Everyone was greeted with a hug and kiss. Young and old came together to have a nice time. The program started and it was a huge success. Pictures were taken and everyone wore their best. Some who we saw that night, we might never see again. But tonight we are just going to have fun and get to know one another again. After we ate, we sang songs together — some from long ago and some from today. Too bad so many of our loved ones are gone now. I just know they would have loved to have seen all of their loved ones together in one room. But as much fun as we were having, it all had to come to an end. Time was up, and we no longer had time to finish having such a good time. After all of the worrying and staying up late, everything turned out so good. Everything was perfect. But the time was up. We had to leave. It took us months to get together, now we didn't want to part. But regardless of how much fun we had, we had to go on our separate ways.

I began to think, "we promise to call or write but we never do. Once we leave this place we might never see our loved ones again". After all of the family left, I just looked around the room because I knew that this day would never come again. But I knew that one day soon, very soon, we might be sitting around thinking about that great reunion. We would wonder what everyone was doing, feeling happy knowing that everyone had a nice time. And probably wondering if anyone could have planned a better reunion than we did. When a sound is heard all over the world, our Father which is in heaven will announce it is time for His GREAT REUNION to start. The trumpets sound. Millions and millions of angels will accompany the Lord in the clouds coming back to this earth to receive all of the people who have been faithful to the Lord. He doesn't have to run all over town trying to find the biggest halls at the best price because He has already made plans — not for just a little hall but He has prepared mansions for His GREAT REUNION.

When Jesus calls for His faithful ones, they don't have to run out and shop for the perfect outfit. When the dead in Christ come forth from their dusty graves and go up to meet the Lord, not only are they given their long white robes but they are given a new body. And the ones who are alive will also be caught up to meet the Lord and will receive their long white robes and also given a new body.

The Lord is not planning a little family outing, but He is planning for all of the faithful that are in the world. The righteous don't have to save to take a trip to another city for their reunion. They have stored up their treasure in heaven and they will be caught up to meet the Lord.

When you see Jesus coming back in the clouds with His angels, what a "family reunion" that will be. You don't have to worry about the time we will have to spend together. We don't have to worry about never seeing each other again because we will be with Christ and His Father forever. What a grand banquet that will be — not just a few family members but so many people you can't begin to count them. You don't have to worry about finding something to eat. You have a tree in the midst of the street that yields twelve different manner of fruits every month. We will meet our father there. We will meet our mother there. Our sisters and brothers will meet us there. Oh what a great reunion that will be. We will talk to Jesus and get to know Him. We will thank Him for being so good to us and thank Him for dying on that cross to save our souls.

We will get to know God. We will get together and sing to the glory of God and His Son. We will sing with great powerful voices and I can't wait to sing my favorite, "We Shall Behold Him Face to Face"! When we get to heaven all of the burdens, all of the worries and all of the heartaches won't mean a thing when we behold Him face to face. When we sit at the feet of Jesus we won't have a care in the world. And the very best part is just when you are having a nice time you don't have to leave and go home. You are already home and you don't have to worry about getting tired because you will never be tired again. We could ask Jesus all of the questions that we need an answer for. Jesus and His Father will gladly answer any questions that we need answered.

You will not see anyone in heaven blind or deaf because Jesus will open the eyes of the blind and unstop the ears of the deaf. You will not see wheelchairs and crutches sitting around heaven because Jesus has healed all of the ones with broken bones and He will strengthen all of our crippled limbs so that we can walk or run if we want to all around heaven. He will heal all types of diseases, so you will only see very healthy people in heaven. There will be no more death there. We will be so happy that there will never be any need of crying again. There will be no crime there. You will never again have to lock a door or shut a window because there will not be any thieves up there. You will never be afraid that someone would harm you, because there will not be guns or knives in heaven. No one would want to be violent there. You never have to worry again about writing a check, paying a bill, or the hustle and bustle of going back and forth to work. Never again will you have to fight the traffic of everyday life. We will have peace there — PERFECT PEACE!

This is the greatest day of our lives. After seeing Jesus and God the Father, and seeing all of the angels all around them, we will meet all of the disciples, even Adam and Eve. We will see all of the things that we have read about in the Bible. What a day that will be!

**THANK YOU LORD FOR ALLOWING US TO ATTEND
THE GREATEST REUNION IN THE WORLD!**

God Is Always in Control

We think of God as being that almighty God who is way up in the Heavens that no one can see. That God who no one can reach. But He's there for us watching us, wanting to help us, loving us. GOD IS ALWAYS IN CONTROL. He knows all things and sees all things. God is always there. God can cause the mighty winds to blow and calms the raging sea. GOD IS ALWAYS IN CONTROL. God blew His breath into man's nostril and man became a living soul. He made the Heavens and earth, and had a plan from the beginning in order to save the world from their sins. GOD IS ALWAYS IN CONTROL. God knows every hair that's on our heads. He knows the day and time when each one of us is born and He knows when our life is over. GOD IS ALWAYS IN CONTROL. You might think that this world is so violent, but God will only let it go so far — then He will step in and stop it because GOD IS ALWAYS IN CONTROL.

God loves us and will never turn His back on us, but we turn our backs on God. Some even curse Him. They are so busy making that almighty dollar that their minds are on worldly things — not God. But, through all of your wealth and fame, you are not happy and you can't find peace until you find Christ for yourself.   Then you will know for yourself that GOD IS ALWAYS IN CONTROL. Man makes plenty of money writing books on how babies are born and they think they know everything. But it is such a mystery how a baby is formed inside of the womb. It grows month after month until its due date, and I don't care how much education your doctor has he cannot tell you exactly when the baby is going to be born. But GOD KNOWS, BECAUSE HE IS ALWAYS IN CONTROL. Do you think that when you go into the hospital and you are sick and you see so many miracles being performed, that you think that is the work of the doctors?

God knows all and He guides the hand of the doctor to make you well. You might give the doctor and hospital the credit, but we know that GOD WAS IN CONTROL. God is never old. Neither is He old-fashioned — although God has been around for centuries. He is RIGHT ON TIME. We serve a God who knows all, and knows everything that is going on in the world. He is not suffering from Alzheimer's. We can never fool God. Sometimes we treat people any way that we want to, say whatever we want to them or dress the way we want to thinking, "Why not!". After all, no one will see us. But we forget that God knows all and sees all because GOD IS ALWAYS IN CONTROL.

Some think that they are gods here on earth, but why would you put your trust in a god that gets sick, and has all types of diseases just like you could get. They get sick and die. Then another earthly god takes his place, and it goes on and on. But people respect and revere him and believe everything that he tells them. But what kind of god is that? How can we serve a god like that. How can we pray to that god to heal us when he will get sick and die just like we do? Just suppose we had a life-threatening crisis in our life and we were depending on one of those gods to help us. And just as we were on our way to ask him for help, we found out that he was rushed to the hospital with a heart attack or stroke or maybe he fell down and broke something. Well, how could he help us when he needed help himself?

People, stop and think about WHO you will serve. The next time you bow down to kiss the hand or foot of man who you give all of your respect and call them god on earth, ask yourself a question, was he able to die on the cross for your sins? Was he able to be resurrected from the grave? NO - - because he is only a man. He was made out of dust just like all of us. But I know the TRUE LOVING GOD, and I can put my trust in Him, because He has proven Himself to me time after time because GOD IS ALWAYS IN CONTROL. We never have to worry about getting used to other gods because Our God will never die and He will never change. He is the same yesterday, today and tomorrow. I don't care how powerful man becomes, he cannot defeat the devil.

But my True God can, and He has defeated him all down through history and will keep us from falling into his traps each time he approaches us. God is the only one who can BECAUSE HE IS ALWAYS IN CONTROL. All we have to do is CALL ON HIM. One day we will be marching home to Glory, and as we see all of the wonders in Heaven and meet the Father and His Precious Son, we will say:

THANK GOD THAT HE HAS ALWAYS BEEN IN CONTROL.

Help

A young woman sat in church. The members looked at her and smiled. No one knew her troubles or her burdens. As she sat there listening to the choir while they sang about the love of God she was thinking how, at one time, she had a relationship with the Lord and wondered how she could get to know Him again. When the preacher stood up to present his sermon, he also preached on God's love for us all and how each and every Christian should be Christ-like and love one another. As he spoke, the young woman throught about all that was on her mind — her children and the bad habits she had fallen into. Oh how she wanted to get out of these habits and get to know Christ again. She wanted to be a real mother to her children. They really deserved the best. But she simply couldn't be her best — not like she is today. But where could she turn? Who should she go to with her problems? Who could she trust not to tell everything or to put her down.

She finally got up enough courage, after the pastor finished speaking and gave his appeal, to stand and ask the church to help her to find Christ and help her learn to be a mother to her children. Oh what a good feeling she had! She just knew that she did the right thing and God had sent her to the right place — where Christ was. She just knew that these good people could help and, by the grace of God, they would. They listened to the young women and promised they would pray and help her all they could. In doing their good deed they sent her to the Community Service and told her that she could find help there. But when the service was over, they all left. No one said goodbye. No one invited her home for Sabbath dinner. She went home alone, but that was alright because in her mind she just knew that the church people would help. She had such a good feeling about going to church today.

She had hoped that the Christians would keep their word and pray for her and help her. But no one came. They didn't call. She heard nothing from them at all. She was so disappointed and felt so all alone.

You see, sometime ago, she had asked the church for help and some of them did pray for her. But it seemed that she was right back in the same situation again — even after praying, crying, and pleading that she would change her life and give her life to Christ. But, again and again, she would make an attempt to try. Each time she would fail. Satan had her trapped and she couldn't find her way out. She felt like they had let her down. The Christians were looking at her physical appearance — the way she was talking and acting. They remembered how she acted before and said among themselves, she isn't serious about changing her life. They were tired of her coming to them again after getting into all kinds of trouble hoping the church would bail her out. They were just tired of it. At one of their church meetings, the subject of the woman was brought up and one of the members remembered what she had told them in confidence some time ago. They told it all. Her past was all brought up that day. After hearing what was going on in her life, the good people decided not to help and just went on their way — back to their busy schedules.

The incident with the young woman was soon forgotten and the church went on as they usually did — singing God's praises and preaching about the love of God. One day, about six months later, the church received word that this woman was found dead in her apartment. She was there alone. When the news was announced to the members they wondered what had happened to her. Immediately they called and visited and did all they could to help the family in their time of grief. Now, that was fine. But the young woman who needed her church was gone. She didn't need their kindness any longer She couldn't smell the flowers, hear a prayer, see a smiling face, or hear her children cry. No one had to do a thing for her now. At last she was at peace.

But what about us Christians? We are still here singing, praying and preaching about the love of God. We are so quick to say, "Amen". We even shout about how good Christ has been to us. We testify how He brought us out of our sins over and over and how we slip right back into the same sins again. Sometimes we get holy and sanctified and we forget where we came from. We no longer see the alcoholic as a person or care about the young girl who is expecting her first baby and feels that she is all alone. Do we think about that person who is in prison for a crime that he has committed? Can we reach out our hand to help that drug addict looking for help or the homeless looking for a place to stay or food to eat? As we look at these poor souls we no longer see Christ in them. We tend to criticize them. We wonder why they can't do better, why they do the things that they do? It just doesn't make any sense to live the way that they do. When will they make something out of themselves? A lot of Christians feel this way because they feel that they are above these problems and they never have to worry about anything like this. How do you think any of us are able to stay firm in the Lord? Only by the grace of God can we make it. If we take our eyes off of Christ, we will fail. If Christ was not in our life we would be that drug addict on the street, that alcoholic in the alley, or maybe in prison.

But Christ in our life makes such a big difference. Now you can sing, "Oh how I love Jesus because He first loved me". Christ provided you with that beautiful home, money in the bank, a nice car, family and a good job. Thank God by helping others. Give to the people who cry out to you for help. Christ sent someone to help you when you were at your lowest point. Let's not forget where we came from. Thank God by reaching out to help someone else. Have a little compassion for others. If the clock could have been turned back and the young woman came to the church for help, they would fast and fall on their knees in prayer for her, put their arms around her in kindness and truly, truly preach Christ to her. What a different that would have made in her life. No matter how many times she came to them for help, "Just Do It!" That's what true Christianity is all about.

Christ is so patient with us. He is always there for us all. You never hear Christ talking about us or putting us down. Let's learn to do the same for your brothers and sisters that are in need. Christ needs us to reach out for His love to the ones who are crying in the darkness. How could you say that you love Christ and walk right past His little ones in need? How could we love Christ and not see Him in the faces of the less fortunate.

Ram In the Bush

Abraham didn't hesitate one minute to offer his only son, Isaac, as a sacrifice to the Lord. But the Lord sent Abraham a ram in the bush before he killed his son. God also provides us with a ram in the bush. A ram, in our case, is not an animal. For example, one day it was very hot outside but I decided to take a walk down to the store. As I was walking, God was trying to show me that it was just too hot for me to take that trip at that time. But I was hardheaded. I kept on walking. I should have turned around and gone back home but I said to myself, "I am this far, I will just keep on going". I had to stop along the way and rest. But I kept on walking. I was getting weaker and weaker. Finally I arrived at the store. I went in and rested. I was so hot but the store felt so cool. I just sat there and cooled off for a while. After I cooled off I felt better, so I brought what I came into the store for. It felt so good inside of the store. Oh how I wished I was home in my nice, cool apartment. But I forgot one thing when I walked to the store, I had to walk back home.

I remembered that my daughter was around the corner at her friend's house, so I tried to reach her but no one was there. So I went outside to start my walk home, when coming toward me was a lady I hadn't seen in a long time. At first I looked, but I didn't think that I knew her. But as she came closer I knew exactly who she was, and we hugged each other and I asked her which way she was going and she said that she would take me home. I said thank you and then I told the Lord thank you, you just sent me a RAM IN THE BUSH! Sometimes we are so stubborn and we want to do things OUR WAY, and we find ourselves in trouble and we can't find our way out. When we do it ourselves, we may start to depend on drugs and alcohol or even sex — trying to do things our way. The next thing we know is our own way has us hooked on drugs or alcohol or committing suicide. Our ways don't work and we may find ourselves at "the end of our rope" with no hope. But the Lord always has a RAM IN THE BUSH to help us, to assist us in finding our way out of a jam, when we are doing things on our own.

It is like a person who has been in a coal mine and, as that person goes from side to side trying to find their way out after bumping from side to side, they find their way out. Suddenly they can see the light that can lead them to safety. That's the same way the Lord does us. When He steps in to help us, He sends us a RAM IN THE BUSH to lead us out of our situations. The Lord sends us someone to help us, someone we can trust, someone who lets the Lord lead his or her life. Remember, God works through people. He sends His people where they are needed. Have you ever gotten yourself in such a jam until you just give up, you blame God, and everybody else except yourself? You might even think that there is not a God. If there was he would never let us get into this fix we're in.

The Father sometimes just stands by. He protects us from too many blows. We might get tossed and turned around in this world but one day, after we have had enough, then we call on the Lord. He hears our cries and steps in to help us by sending us that RAM THAT HE HAS IN THE BUSH TO HELP US and that's all that we need to turn our lives around. Always remember that God will never let so many burdens be put on us that we can't bare. We always have a friend in God. No one stands by us like our Heavenly Father! No one loves us like Him! We might think that we have everything in the world that we might ever need but, if you don't have Jesus, you don't have anything! He's all that we need! Thank you Jesus, for that RAM IN THE BUSH!

Faith of a Mustard Seed

The Lord said, if we have the FAITH OF A MUSTARD SEED it can remove mountains (Mark 11:22-23). We read these words and never stop to think about what the words mean. FAITH is the substance of things hoped for, the evidence of things not seen (Heb. 11:1). The Lord tells us to have FAITH — the FAITH of a tiny MUSTARD SEED. We don't have to have millions of dollars, be so beautiful, or be the smartest person in the world for the Lord to do good things for us. He said just have FAITH the size of a MUSTARD SEED. When you put just one seed in your hand you can barely see it, but the Lord tells us to have the FAITH of a MUSTARD SEED. That means when I need to have to STEP OUT ON FAITH, the only thing I have to do is to trust in the Lord with all of my heart and know that the Lord will make everything alright in my life.

WE NEED TO KEEP OUR MINDS CLEAR so that we can hear that still small voice that is speaking to us. A lot of times we ask God for something and, like a little child, we want it right then. But, sometimes, we have to wait. Well, that's when FAITH in God works. When we ask God for something, and we have FAITH that God has promised us that all that we need IS the FAITH of a MUSTARD SEED and we know that is enough to move mountains — NOTHING CAN STOP US. God has promised us that is all that we need. The Lord is so good! He doesn't demand that we jump over hoops to please Him. He doesn't demand that we walk through fire or cut ourselves to prove to Him that we love Him. All we have to do is to have FAITH the size of a MUSTARD SEED.

Have you evern seen plants grow? When you dig up the ground, you dig deep and put in a few seeds and cover them up. When they come up you are amazed at the fields and fields of beautiful crops as far as the eye can see. Just think what happens when you give your life over to the Lord. First He digs down deep into our souls and cleans out all of the sins and corruption that has built up inside of us. Then He plants GOOD SEEDS — like FAITH, HOPE, CHARITY and LOVE. All we have to do is to believe that the Lord can remove mountains. When we believe in the Lord, we will not let anything or anybody come into our path and turn us around. Trust in the Lord with all of your heart. Nothing that you have or will ever receive could compare with the Love of God. When you put your trust in the Lord, you will be surprised what good things could happen in your life.

Sometimes the Lord touches the hearts of others and, to your surprise, someone is there to come to your rescue. For example when you are at the grocery store, and the cashier rings up your groceries and you are a little "short", you search your pockets or purse for that extra money to pay for your groceries. The cashier is standing there waiting patiently for you to get the money. By now, the line is getting longer and longer. Suddenly, you realize you don't have the money to pay for your groceries and you start going through your bags to see what you can put back when you hear a voice in the back of you asking the cashier, "How much does she owe?" You turn around and see the woman in back of you giving the cashier the amount of money you owed. You thank the lady and can't believe that person helped you, but you forgot that the Lord is with you — no matter what you need. He is there to help you.

Like so many elderly people who feel so all alone, always remember you have a Heavenly Father who is always there for you. He has not brought you this far to leave you. He sometimes sends someone to cook you a meal or help you with whatever problem you might have. The Lord is there for us. He is there to help us with or through whatever it is that we need. We can always count on Him. Sometimes you have to move out of your apartment to give another person a place to live, but one thing you forget is you can't afford the larger apartment. What do you do? Do you throw up your hands in disgust? Or do you apply your FAITH and leave those bills to the Lord? Because you have the FAITH of a MUSTARD SEED you will see that all of your bills are paid and you don't have to have a care in the world BECAUSE YOU HAVE JESUS IN YOUR LIFE.

THAT'S ALL YOU NEED!

Our Children Need Our Help!

When I was a child I spoke as a child. I ran, played and walked as a child. I didn't have a care in the world. Everything seemed perfect. My friends and I played games like "Cops and Robbers" or Cowboys and Indians". We would have "play" guns and, when we would shoot at each other, we would fall down and "play" dead. At the end of the game whoever had fallen down would get up and would start again. The girls would "play" mothers and have tea parties. We would take good care of our doll babies. We would feed them, change their diapers, and put them on clean clothes. To us that was a fun day. When we were finished, we would put our dollies in the corner and start playing something else. We would sit and talk about what we would become when we grew up. We all agreed that we would have a family — maybe become doctors, nurses or lawyers or fulfill any dream that we might have.

Our children have so many problems in their lives today. We interviewed some teenagers about life and their views on all of the violence all around them. The first teenager who was interviewed said, "As a young child, I felt as though I was loved by my family. I had a way of getting whatever I wanted from my parents because that was the way that they showed me that they loved me, but I was never disciplined by either one of them. So, as a small child, I could do whatever I wanted to and I would never get into trouble. As the years went on, I became out of control. I wish my parents had taught me right from wrong when I was young so I would know how to cope with life today.

I think that kids reach out for gangs when they feel that they don't have anyone to love them or they don't have anywhere to go. Some kids have parents who are always yelling at them or putting them down. Gangs make kids feel that they are important, that they are loved, that they are part of a family. They make you believe that they understand what you are going through. Before you know it you are caught up in something that you can't get yourself out of — short of death.

One thing I would like to tell teens is whatever you do, talk to your parents, pastor, or counselor about problems. Please, please don't seek out a gang. That is not the way out. Fighting and killing are not the way out. Stealing and taking drugs are not the way out. I have found Christ Jesus in my life. I have learned to pray now. I don't feel so all alone. I still have problems because I brought them on myself and I know I have to work them out myself. No one else can help me with my problems but God. I don't feel so all alone anymore. I go to Jesus and ask Him, Dear Lord, please help me. And He will take my hand and guide me through my problems".

Our second teen said, "My mother just doesn't take the time to listen to my problems. I know that she has problems of her own but sometimes I just need her to let me know that she cares for me, and stop treating me as if I was a little child. I need her to trust me. I want her to see that I am growing up". I would like to tell young people that sex is not all that it is cracked up to be. Before you think about having sex, talk to your parents or other adults that you trust. Boys should be taught that girls must be respected. They are not just a sex object. Girls must stop thinking about having a boyfriend. Keep your mind on your studies.

Learn to know yourselves and to love yourselves. I would hate to get pregnant and have to drop out of school or end up with aids and die at a young age so I want to tell other young people, don't get hooked on drugs and gangs. Stay in school. You don't need guns or knives in your pockets to make you a big shot. The only thing that you need is Jesus. Carry the 'good book', the Bible. That is all of the ammunition that you need. Remember you only have one life to live, so live it to the fullest".

Our third teenager said, "My mother and I don't have a very good relationship. We don't talk a whole lot. She doesn't seem to understand me and, sometimes, I don't understand myself. As a child I had a lot of problems but now I am growing up, and I want to make something out of my life. Nowadays you are afraid to have a fight or have an argument with someone, because if you argue or fight the next thing you know someone pulls out a gun or knife and you might get yourself killed or crippled for life. To me it just isn't worth it. Some of my friends want to be pregnant because they want someone to love them or some believe the lies that their boyfriends tell them and want to have a baby for them.

There is no glamour in getting pregnant. It is something to trap you. Wait until you are grown to bring a baby into the world. I like to tell young people to stay away from drugs, because drugs dull the mind and could cause violence that leads to death. Put your focus on God and get your education. Take your time and focus on your future". Our fourth teenager said, "As a young child I felt as though I was on my own. My mom was not there for me as much as she should have been. I felt that my life was so screwed up. I would watch her go through a lot of changes in her life, but now she has changed her life. My life was so screwed up but now I see things in a whole new light. My father was never in the home, so I don't know how it would have been with him in the home.

With so much violence in the world today I hate to hear about kids joining gangs and killing up each other day after day. I hate to see girls get pregnant at a young age. They have so much life to live. You can't have fun with a baby by your side". The fourth teenager continued, "I think about my own life, and I pray to God that He makes me strong, that I get my education so I can get a good job, and keep the desire to make something out of myself. Jesus loves you young people. Let Him in your life!" I would like to stop here and add a little note. I am an older adult. I have children and grandchildren of my own. The world around me today frightens me. The way our young people are living their lives makes me very sad. Our young boys (you have to call them boys because they are not old enough to vote or drive a car), are dying each and every day by the hands of other teens who are not old enough to vote or drive a car. Our young girls are playing with dolls one day and, next, are pregnant with babies of their own. Girls are now having to quit school, get on welfare, have no education nor any future.

Our fifth teenager said, "I was a happy child. I thought that everything was going fine until one day my mother decided that she no longer wanted to live with my father and we moved out to our own apartment. I used to wonder why we left. I don't care because my father and I have a good relationship and that's all that matters. We love each other and I know that he is always in my corner. We moved from city to city, and I didn't meet a lot of people. But I saw a lot of gangs and kids on drugs just hanging around getting into trouble. I decided that I didn't want to get involved in that type of life. I had no one to talk to so I kept a lot of things to myself. I would just cry a lot. Sometimes I would visit a family member and I would tell this family member everything that was on my mind. Everyone needs someone to talk to. We moved to a new place and I had to meet new friends. I had a fight or two — sometimes you just have to prove yourself to other kids. I think about the fights now that I am older and I know I would have handled the situation differently.

I had some bad experiences in my life and I think that because of my experiences I have become a stronger person for it. I have seen what happens to a person who drinks alcohol and takes drugs into their bodies. I will not hang around them because I never want to take a chance on anyone getting me hooked on drugs or alcohol. I see the violence in our teens' lives today, and the adults all seem to blame the kids. But sometimes I feel that it's the adults' fault for the violence in our kids. Sometimes the kids have so much going on at home with their parents that they don't know how to cope with their problems, so they are walking around with a time bomb inside. And, when the first thing happens to them outside of the home, they explode. They start fighting over nothing. They will shoot you or stab you at a drop of a hat, and don't even care what happens to the person. They get involved with gangs — trying to fit in. They find themselves in trouble with the law or other gang members and they either end up in jail or dead.

Young girls need to be educated about their bodies. They need to learn that they are not a baby machine. They need to respect themselves, and the young boys need to learn to respect the young girls. I don't keep things on my mind that I can't do anything about. A lot of kids go through a lot of pain and suffering but there is no reason for them to go through that by themselves. Please get help! Either talk to your parents or other adults who you can trust. If they don't get the help that they need, they will have a breakdown. Sometimes you might have to cry about what is bothering you.

Believe in God. He is always there to help you. I read in my Bible that the Lord has promised us that we should bring our burdens to Him and leave them there. That's what I am striving to do. When I get upset I sit down and write whatever comes to mind and that makes me feel better. Our sixth teenager said, "My father, like a lot of black males, doesn't want the responsibility of supporting his children. This puts a big strain on my mother who tries to do it all. When I see her upset, I get so angry that I just want to do something to get even with him — not something crazy, but just get even. He doesn't treat his children the same. I wish that my father would realize that we need him in our lives too. My mother is my right hand. She is always there for me when I need her. She treats us all the same. I believe that she loves all of us alike. When I am away from home, I am scared. Anyone could just drive by and shoot me. I always say a little prayer before I leave home. I believe that God will protect me. Teen groups can help young people stay out of trouble, as well as sports. But the best advice that I know to give other teens is to get Christ in your life and see what a difference it will make".

Our seventh teenager said, "When I was a child, life was a lot different. You could run and play and have fun. You could go anywhere and not worry about anything. But, as I reached my teens, life started getting serious. So many pressures face me now — like finding a job, picking a college, making a decision on whether or not to attend college. Whatever I decide will effect my life forever. I can no longer run home to mother when I have a problem. I have to rely on the teaching that she provided me through the years". Young males have so many pressures in their lives. It seems that it is harder for them to keep their mind on their studies. If you don't finish school and graduate, you could ruin any chance that you might have to survive in this world".

The seventh teenager continued, "The male family member who was in my life was not my father, but he was there for me. I try to avoid trouble by not getting myself into arguments. But, if someone calls me out, I will have to fight, and I don't want that because now people don't fight fair. They will come back and shoot me or a member of my family. I never want to put my family in this type of trouble. I feel that girls are not looking for a nice clean-cut guy in their lives. They want someone who others think is good looking and is well built, and the girls don't care how they are treated as long as they can say, 'this is my man'.

Every young person needs a role model in their lives — someone who will take an interest in what goes on in your life. For example, I lost someone very dear to me and although I had to go on with my life, I think about this special person. When I attempt to do wrong, I think about that special person and I say to myself, what would this special person think about me if I do this thing — and that stops me from doing just anything. Sometimes parents are blamed for what their children are doing. Most of the time, parents don't even know where their children are. Young people, talk to your parents! Get your education! You need to learn more about life because there is more in life than getting pregnant and joining a gang. If you will learn God's word, it will keep you from the temptations of life".

Our eighth teenager said, "I was taught how to study from the elementary school that I attended. Sometimes teachers really do make a difference. I think that teenage girls are confused about life. They feel that to be popular they have to have a boyfriend and they let him treat her anyway that he wants to and she accepts it. They think that having a baby is a way to get someone to love them, but the baby traps them. They can't go anywhere or do anything without their baby. I want to tell young people to think before they put that weapon into their pocket. Think of the consequences and make sure that you are willing to pay the price. You spend your time trying to be popular. With your record, you are well known to the police or to other gang members. Is that what you want? Young people, stay in school! Don't get caught up with drugs or violence. Have a normal childhood and be a teenager as long as you can, because when you grow up you can never get those years back".

Martin Luther King once said in a speech, "I had a dream that one day my poor little children will one day be judged, not by the color of their skin but by the content of their characters". He wanted to see his people have equal opportunities in this world we live in today. But some of his people believe that the best way to accomplish their goal is to join a gang, talk tough, or by getting high on anything that they can get their hands on. They are not only taking drugs themselves but are selling them to small children and pregnant girls — and babies are born hooked on drugs or children born with aids. Our young boys have only one thing to look forward to — that is to kill or be killed. I don't think this was the message that Martin Luther King had in mind for his people.

Our ninth teenager told the following story. "When I was a child I always had problems listening to my parents, so I would run away a lot. I gave them a lot of troubles. We moved around the city a lot. I remember one place we moved into I met a few drug dealers who encouraged me to become a drug dealer by telling me how much money I could make. I started hanging around with gang members thinking that was the only way that I could survive. If I had enough people with me and, if I carried a weapon, you had nothing to worry about. At any time day or night there were people coming there to buy drugs, or you would hear screams from someone getting shot or stabbed. Ambulances and police cars were always in the neighborhood. We would get together with other gang members and have a fight. Of course we had knives and guns and it became our own little war zone. I wouldn't listen to the advice that my parents tried to give me, but I would listen to other older people who happened to be drug dealers. They would tell me how great I was and show me how much money I could make. I really thought that I was important".

He continued to pour out his heart and said, "Then I started smoking drugs and trying to sell drugs. My friends and I would steal money from people and, if they didn't like it, we would beat them up and never thought about them again. One night my whole life was changed. That night, I got arrested and the judge gave me a few months in juvenile center. It really taught me a lot. I am older. I now realize I should have listened to my parents. They only wanted the best for me. Now we talk about our problems together. We try to work them out with God's help. I have younger relatives and friends and we play football and basketball. I tell them that their parents know best and to listen to them. I try to steer them straight and show them that there is more in life than drugs and gangs. Selling drugs might look like good money but it only leads you to death or jail. I want to be a better person for my little child. My child has made me a better person. I have become a better person because I am a father".

Our tenth teenager said, "I know that I cause my mom a lot of problems. Sometimes she is so short-patient with me. I think that she does the best that she can. In the school that I attend, it seems that every time you look up there is another girl pregnant. It seems that these girls do not have a mind of their own. They look pitiful walking the halls. They look so young to be pregnant. They can hardly get around from class to class. Young boys don't care. I know that they see how miserable they have made the young girl's life. They just go from girl to girl trying to see how many they can 'get'. What they don't seem to understand is that this pregnancy will produce a real live baby who needs to be fed, and they will need clothes and Pampers. This child has to be taken care of twenty-four hours a day. The child needs a father and mother in its life. Young people remember, when you decide to have sex, the responsibility that comes with it will last a lifetime".

We, as adults, need to rally around our children and give them the love that they need. I have seen mothers and some fathers, struggling trying to work and raise their children. Because the mother is so stressed out and feels so all alone trying to raise these children, the children pick up the "sense" that the mother is not always able to handle things so the children take advantage of the situation and become very wild and out of control. The mother sometimes doesn't know which way to turn. The mother gives the children all the advice that she can, but the child doesn't listen to a word that she tells them. But they will listen to whatever anyone else tells them, and the next thing that the mother knows her child is in trouble with the law. Now she has to run around trying to raise money to keep her child out of jail. Though it is too late, the child finally wants to hear what the mother has to say.

The way the kids are today is that one minute they are leaving the house, the next report that you receive is that your child is dead — killed by the hands of another child with a gun. The mother is grieved that her child is gone. She will never see her child again on this earth. She has an emptiness in her heart. Her young girls are slipping out at night after she has gone to bed, running after these young boys and the next thing you know she is telling her that she is pregnant and the boy is nowhere to be found. Now the mother not only has to take care of her children, she now has grandchildren to care for because, in most cases, the girls are not old enough to be a mother. The parent is struggling trying to care for her family.

We need to find a way to help the parents. The parents need an extra hand to take care of their children. Sometimes Christians just stand back and shake their heads and say, "That's too bad. I wish I could help". They sing their songs, pray their prayers, and go to their homes and do nothing. We need to visit the homes and teach the children about the love of God by showing them that you love them, that adults do understand, and they do care.

We feel so generous at Christmas or Thanksgiving time, but we need to show the love of Christ to a young person by loving them. Let's work in our neighborhoods. We need to find a way to protect our children. Remember they are our future. What we plant in them today will "grow up"in them as adults. Young people, put your trust in the Lord and He will see you through.

A Birthday Wish

Today I celebrated another birthday. They seem to come around so quickly now. I wonder where did all of the years go? What have I accomplished in my lifetime? When you are very young, you can't wait to become an adult. But, once you are over thirty, the years just seem to fly by. As a child, I would sit and try to figure out how old I would be in the year 1960. That was okay because I would be an adult. Then I added up to see my age in the years 1970 and 1980 — and then I came to the year 1990. I wondered what I would be doing — if I would have a family, have a good job, live in a big house, or if I would have money. When I stepped over from childhood into adulthood, I would write things down as to what I wanted to be doing as an adult. If I made a mistake I could take an eraser and rub it out, and start all over again. But in real life, you can't do that. I have made many mistakes in my life. Some I just had to take in stride and try to do my best. Others I could put behind me and move on. I learned great lessons from my experiences in life.

Sometimes I stop and ask myself, why did I do the things that I did? Life sometimes throws you from side-to-side, like you are on a roller coaster, and you can't seem to find your way out. In my life I have found a friend, a true friend. I turned away from Christ and it took me a long time to find my way back to Him. Even though I made mistakes and turned away from him in my life, He always kind-of softened the blows. HE WAS ALWAYS THERE FOR ME! I think it took me a long time to realize that JESUS NEVER LEFT ME and I WAS NEVER ALONE. I know now I could never survive without Christ in my life. There is a quotation that I heard my son use down in the park. I don't know who wrote it but it is so true: "MEET ME, FORGET ME, YOU HAVE MISSED NOTHING. MEET CHRIST, FORGET HIM, YOU HAVE LOST EVERYTHING". How true that statement is. You can always count on Him. Your family might not always be on your side. Your friends might leave you. But CHRIST WILL BE WITH YOU TO THE END.

One of the good things about getting older is you can tell others about your experiences in life. No one knows better than you what you have gone through. Everyone has an experience they have gone through in their lives — something no one else might ever know about but you and God. I believe that we are given a past. It we didn't have a past, how would we grow? Because we have a past, that will help keep us humble. I always thought in the back of my mind that, if I had not made a name for myself or a lot of money by a certain age, then I felt that I would never make it. I thought that it would be all over for me. Well, that was the way I felt when I was very young. Now that I am older, I realize that at any age you can learn something. At any age, you can enjoy life.

Everyone is looking for love in their lives, and every time you have a birthday I think you kind-of panic and wonder if you will ever find that special person in your life. The ones who are married kind-of wonder if their mate will still love them and find them attractive as they grow older. Christ doesn't think about us as being old. Really, we are like small children — according to the Bible. People who were called "old" back then were living to be 600 and 800 years old. They were still fathering children and in good health. They were not like us today — all broken down and needing help to get along. MY BIRTHDAY WISH IS: Let's not worry about how old you are. Don't sit around counting the gray hairs and trying to hide the bald spot on top. Those are just some of the signs of getting older and, by the time you get used to being the age that you are, guess what — it's time for another birthday and you are another year older.

Live the time that you have to the fullest. Enjoy your life. Find some kind of activity or travel. But, whatever you do, ENJOY YOUR LIFE. Don't let anyone tell you that you are too old to enjoy your life. I would like to see everyone, young or old, find the Lord in their life. That's what we need in these times. Give the Lord ALL of the Glory. Thank Him for seeing us through another birthday. Through Jesus we have experienced true love. He has been there with us through our whole life. FALL IN LOVE WITH JESUS and do all to the Glory of God. Then we will learn to be thankful for all of the years that the Lord grants us!

General Inspection

Today, in our apartment complex, we received a letter from the owners informing us of their plans to inspect our units. Everything had to be in top condition and, if it wasn't, we would be asked to move. They gave us the date and the time when they would be arriving. They allowed us a couple of weeks before they arrived. Some started right away clearning walls, washing windows, cleaning venetian blinds, cleaning carpets, rearranging cabinets, etc. They were cleaning all the way up until the due date. Others waited until the week that they were coming to start getting things in order — cleaning up all through the night trying to have everything right. The ones that started early didn't have to rush too much. They could do a little at a time. Others that waited until the last minute had to rush and worked all night. Now comes the day that the owners arrive to inspect.

You listen as the men knock on each door. You listen as they get closer to your door. It seems that they were in each apartment for a long time. Then, finally, they arrive at your door. You hear the man yell out, "I am the inspector, coming to inspect your apartment!" After you let him in, he goes from room to room looking everywhere at the windows, floors, cabinets, and bathrooms. You are right behind him watching him check everything. Then he tells you that everything is just fine.. You thank him, as he moves on to another apartment and you thank God for letting everything be okay. You think about all of the work that you had to do to make sure that the house was in top condition. And how about the money you had to pay out for cleaning materials. It costs quite a lot.

When I had settled down after the inspection, I started thinking about another inspection that we will have. It will be one very big inspection — one that could cause us to not only lose our apartments, but our eternal life. We have always read in the Bible to be ready. You know neither the day or hour in which the son of Man cometh in the clouds. And you can't wait until He comes to get ready. You have to start now. It takes time to get to know the Lord. We are given message after message that the Lord is coming. The landlord only had to write us one letter and we obeyed him right away. But God has to send us all kinds of warnings about His return. We just go on as though we have years and years to get ready.

Let's say when we received the letter from the owners that we read it and just threw it in the trash and didn't even think about it again. What do you think would happen when the day came for the inspection and your apartment was not ready? You hear a knock on the door. You try to clean up very quickly, hiding things everywhere before you let the person in. You open the door and tell the man to come on in. But now it is too late. that's not only the way it will be but only worse when Jesus comes back to this earth. In Revelation, Jesus tells us that He will come back as a thief in the night — be ye always ready.

Jesus has taught us about His love. He has proven His love for us, time after time. And the only thing that we have to do is to obey, put our trust in the Lord and He will see you through anything. He will give you life everlasting. No matter what goes on in your life, you have Jesus. We treat Jesus any way. We take Him for granted. We say, "Oh I love the Lord but I can't stop living my life now. Maybe later I will give my life to the Lord". Each and everyday we wake up, Jesus has to take care of us. When we make it through the day, Jesus had to oversee our lives. But we don't even give that a thought. He really doesn't have to protect us if He didn't want to. But He loves us so much. It hurts Him when we turn our back on Him. When we don't do the will of the Lord, we live our lives doing whatever we want to do and never giving the Lord a thought until we get into trouble. Then we remember Him. He reaches out and helps us again. This happens time after time — never building up trust in God, never asking His forgiveness. Then one day it will be too late. It won't be the inspector at the door, it will be Jesus and it will be too late.

When we keep the commandments of God and have faith in Him we are building up our treasures in heaven, loving the Lord and putting our trust in Him. One day when He returns in the clouds, we will be waiting with open arms because we have been watching and praying for the day that we will be with the Lord. And when He inspects our lives His Father will not see us standing before Him, He will see His precious Son. And we will hear Him say, "Well done my good and faithful servant. You have been faithful over a few things and I will make you ruler over many".

Three More Pies

On December 21, we the members of the Bright and Morning Star Ministry decided to have a little treat for the people in the park. It feels so good being with the people in the park. They have so much faith that it sometimes puts us to shame. Each and every week we are in the park feeding the people. Larry is spreading the gospel and praying for them because they have a problem. We want to put their problems in the blessed hand of Jesus. The Bible said we will have the poor with us always. When Jesus has blessed us so much we are not to sit back and act like we did it on our own, but we are to reach down to help the less fortunate and pick them up just like Christ did when He walked on this earth. He helped the sick and poor. He always gave them hope, had compassion for all, and he fed them because Jesus would never let His people go hungry. We are supposed to be like Jesus in our lifetime. Sometimes we could be entertaining angels and never ever know it. We have to be very careful who we turn away.

When you look into the faces of your brothers and sisters, you are looking into the face of Christ. How can you say that you love the Lord who you have never seen and hate your neighbor that you see everyday? When you come across a person — sick or poor — without a place to stay, do what you can to help them. Speak an encouraging word. Tell them how much Jesus loves them and that He will hear their prayers. Now, back to my story. We had planned a very nice dinner for them right before Christmas. We had green beans, parsley potatoes, and barbecue chicken. It was very good. But the real surprise was the pies. We started asking church members, friends and family to make us some sweet potato pies. We asked them early in the month. And on December 21 we started getting calls early telling us that the pies were ready and, thank the Lord, we ended up with 48 sweet potato pies. Thank the Lord. Don't tell me that God doesn't answer prayers. My sister was cutting the pies. We had so many we kept them in the van. She kept calling for three more pies and the children kept them coming. The people ate all that they wanted. No one was turned down.

THANK YOU LORD FOR MAKING THE DAY SO PERFECT!

Whisper a Little Prayer

I love the job that we have taken on each week — cooking for the homeless in the park. Oh, what a great feeling it is to see the people line up to eat what we have cooked that week. You know, the people make you feel so good because no matter what you have they are so thankful. It is not like in our churches where you work so hard and the people are not thankful. They seem to take us for granted. But down in the park, they are really appreciative for what we cook and that we take the time to come down to help them.

Dear Jesus, I want to offer up this little prayer. I am not bragging Lord, not looking for a medal. But Jesus, we worked so hard to make the food just right for the people. Lord sometimes we worked very, very late cooking, cooling and storing the food. Lord you know that we don't have enough room to store the food but, Jesus, you helped us so much. I just don't know what we would do without you. One Saturday we had chicken and noodles and, believe it or not, they spoiled. I think I cried all evening. I just couldn't understand what had happened. But Lord, we didn't give up. Each week, meal after meal, we worked very hard fixing their meals. When we first started we had to take pots downtown with our food in them but, now Jesus, you have provided us with three coolers to keep the food hot. You helped us get a freezer.

At first, we were using the church's pots. Now Lord, we have two very large pots. We found a place where we brought two of the best pots we ever had. Now Lord we have a table, three coolers to keep food hot, one cooler for cold drinks, and utensils heavy enough to stir any size pots. We have plenty of bowls, plates, spoons, forks and cups and we thank you Lord. Just about two weeks ago we had chicken, gravy and rice. Our meat spoiled. The rice and gravy were very good. But, you know, the people thanked us and praised the Lord for what we had brought. What an uplift for our hearts. While we were throwing the meat away we thought about how long it took us to cook the food, then warm it up and clean up. We know that sometimes Satan has to stick his ugly head in the plan. But Jesus, we know that you are stronger than anything Satan can mingle up. Jesus we really believe that YOU are in our plans, and we always want to put YOU FIRST in our lives.

People, you just don't know what the homeless really go through. When we go home, we have a place to go to. We have furniture, a bed to lay on, a kitchen to cook in any time you want to. You can buy and eat anything you want. The people in the park don't have a home to go to or food to eat. They have to depend on soup kitchens for their meals. We must thank God for the kitchens but that is not a home-cooked meal, and that is what we try to cook for them at least once a week. And if they don't make it to the drop-in center by a certain time, they have to sleep anywhere they can — winter or summer. Although they seem hopeless the Lord still hears their cry, and He sends people like us who are willing to help. And Jesus, sometimes we don't even know how we are going to get enough money to fill the pots but YOU have never failed us yet. Thank you, Lord, so very much. I do believe that the work downtown has brought us closer together with you and with each other.

Dear Jesus, help our ministry get stronger. Help us to never start bragging about the work that we do. Help us always to be humble and know that WITHOUT YOU we can do nothing. Lord, you have everything. Help us to help your people wherever we find them. Jesus, please continue to take care of your people in the park — please keep them warm. Lord, thank you for the people through the years who helped us with the food, money and ideas for menus to keep the pots full. I want to whisper this little prayer to ask you Father to please let us continue to fill the pots from week to week. Let the pots be filled just like we are cooking for royalty — the very best that we can cook.

Dear Jesus, please don't let our pots spoil again. Please, Father, guide and protect us in everything that we do for the people. Jesus, you promised us that if we will come to you and ask in Your name, you would grant it. Jesus we have all of the faith in you and we believe that you will grant us the things that we need to carry on your work.

IN THE NAME OF JESUS CHRIST WE PRAY, AMEN.

A Little Touch of Heaven

Last Sabbath, after having a real blessed Sabbath Day, I went to my daughter's house to start warming up the food that we had prepared to feed the homeless in Washington Park. This is what we usually do on Sabbath afternoon, but this Sabbath was different from any other one. My sister, daughter's son and me were running a bit late. But my other son, Larry, had gone on ahead of us. We arrived in the park and our other group of saints were already preparing to feed the people there. The people were lining up as we pulled up and finished unloading the car. As we walked into the park, all of the workers stopped working and we hugged and kissed each other. It made me stop and wonder is this what God meant when He said, "Love one another as I have loved you". Because that day I really felt God's presence there. We really loved one another. It's not hard to love family members or church members and friends. But is it as easy to love outsiders — people of different races or poor people?

We have a crowd of people each week and, praise God, the people have enough to eat. They even have seconds. We all work together as a team. When the people see us working together they don't see black or white, rich or poor there, they only see Christ there — ONLY THE LOVE OF CHRIST IN US. When Jesus said, "I was hungry and you gave me no meat", what would your answer be? Are we too busy to take a minute to see about Jesus' loved ones? When you help someone less fortunate than yourself, you forget about your own problems. You feel so good it's like a little bit of Heaven. I just know Jesus and his angels are there with us, all of us working as a team. We could not work like we do if we didn't have the love of Christ in our hearts. There is love for one another, love for the people and, most of all, love for God. After praying, singing, and testifying Larry gave a short sermonette. I believe that day Jesus showed us a LITTLE TOUCH OF HEAVEN — not the poor people, or the sick people nor the black or white people. But it was the togetherness of people regardless of race or religious preference. We all have one goal.

WE LOVE THE LORD WITH ALL OUR HEARTS,
AND WE LOVE THE PEOPLE.

Our Future

It is almost like a dream. One day we will wake up and our country will be run by our children. That is our future! When they grow up, they will be our future. Now they are boys and girls but, someday, they will grow up and become men and women and what is in them today is going to become worse when they are grown. Have you even stopped and wondered who we will be leaving our country to? "Maybe", you would think, "as old as I am I don't have to worry about the future because I will probably be dead". But, in case you haven't noticed, senior citizens live much longer. They are outliving our young children and young adults! And they will be the ones to take care of you in the future. Stop and look around you! What do you see? Our young children are on drugs and selling them. We are not talking about teens only! We are also talking about small children! They are in school or on the playground selling other young children drugs! Parents are missing money and they would never suspect their little sons or daughters of stealing their money.

A lot of times, parents are too busy to notice a difference in their child. Children are now raising themselves. So they get involved with gangs. Our young teens are doing everything! Their minds are so messed up, they will do anything for drugs. They steal and kill. They think they are so grown up that they can do whatsoever they want to and, when they get caught, they want to cry that they are minors. But our children have become so out of control that we have to do something to help them before it is too late. We are into "Black awareness". We are trying to help our young to succeed in life. First, we need to teach them that the world doesn't owe them anything. And, if they don't work for it, they don't get it. Our home life has changed so much some children are not safe in their own homes. They are not safe from their natural parents, the ones who bore them. Sometimes they are beaten black and blue. There is no love and prayer in the home anymore.

In our schools, prayer has been taken out. The schools say that we no longer need it. Children now come to school with guns and knives — not books! They don't come to learn but to see who has on the most name-brand clothes and shoes. They sell drugs right inside of our schools. Schools have to have detectors in them to try to keep out the drug dealers. But drug dealers are just interested in making a quick buck. They don't think about the childrens' lives that they are ruining with drugs. They are not thinking about the young women who are pregnant and running around looking for the drug dealer every time they find a dollar. And the drug dealer thinks that he is the most important person in the world flashing diamonds and big, shiny cars around — wearing expensive and the best name-brand clothes and shoes. He makes sure all the young children see him — and they worship him.

The gangs are where our children get together and they kill each other. They carry guns just like the Old West. They can get a gun anywhere and as many as they want. Even children are using guns. If someone gets in their way, they just shoot them and never look back. They don't seem to have any feelings. They want to shoot first and then cry that they are underage and should be treated as a child. Our young girls are having babies so fast that it is like babies having babies. The schools have to include nurseries so that the young girls can finish school. The young fathers don't have anything to do with the girl or their baby so the young girl and her little baby are all alone.

Now the young mother has the responsibility of taking care of a very small child who cannot do anything for itself. It happens so often that doctors and counselors have to show films to young girls about what happens when they are careless and listen to all of the promises that the young men tell them. When they stop using their heads and let their guard down, they open the door to trouble thinking that the young men love them. The are unprotected and, in only a few minutes, they can end up pregnant or with aids. Either way their lives are over or different. Once they made that decision, their lives are changed forever.

We are into 'BLACK AWARENESS". We want our children to know their roots — to know where they come from. But one thing they have known is the way we live our lives today will carry on to the future. We no longer put Christ in our lives. We no longer need prayer in the home or school. We can see each and every day how Satan is ruining our young people. Let's put our arms around them before it is too late. Let them know how much we love them. God is so good! He loves our children and wants them to know Him and trust Him.

Parents, when your children are walking around with earphones in their ears, stop sometimes and check what they are listening to. You have no idea what is coming through those earphones. One day, I was in the parking lot and a young man pulled up and the rap music coming out of his C.D. shocked me. The words that were coming out were so shameful that, when he saw me, he did turn it down. But, when your child has on those earphones, you don't know what they are listening to. And you don't know what some of the artists are putting into their young minds. And these suggestions are going over and over in their mind all night because they are listening to their C.D.'s all night.

We have tried everything to get back in control of our children. The more they teach birth control, the more our young girls get pregnant. The more detectors they bring into schools and the more chains they put on the doors, the more guns and knives our children bring into the classrooms. The first thing the authorities want to do is to change leadership. And, when that doesn't work, they call in the therapist who tries but they don't always have all of the answers. But, sometimes, we as parents just sit back and let a stranger tell us what's best for our children. We have taken Christ out of our children's lives. We no longer have time for devotion. We have to show our children that we love them —

teach them about the love of Christ. Children need to be disciplined. They need to be given rules to follow. Take charge of your children! Love them, talk to them and teach them to love the Lord. They can always count on Him all of their lives. Teach them to pray to the Lord everyday of their lives — now and in the future. Teach them that the Lord is always on their side and He will never let them down. WORSHIP HIM young people! This is our future! Our only future is to keep Christ in your life.

JESUS IS THE ANSWER FOR THE FUTURE!
HE IS OUR ONLY HOPE!

Thank you Lord!

Dear Heavenly Father, I don't know exactly how to put into words how I really feel about you. You know that old saying, "Lord you know my heart". I know that you do. I know that you know everything about me. You even know the number of hairs that are on my head. I know that you love me. Sometimes I feel that I might be all alone, and I have felt that no one cares. And then I read just how much you loved me. You laid down your life that I might be saved. I want to say, "THANK YOU!" And then you gave me the Holy Spirit to comfort me. When I am lonely and have a lot of problems on my mind, I just want to say, "THANK YOU LORD!" I know sometimes that I might take you for granted. I don't mean to Father. Sometimes in my daily routine I might say a harsh word to someone or maybe missed someone I could have witnessed to but I didn't. Then there might be someone I should have visited but I was too busy. Forgive me Father for my shortcomings. I know that I must trust you Lord. I read how patient you were with your disciples and other people around you when you were on this earth. That's the way I want to be with people that I meet. I want to be a loving person with my children and my grandchildren. Sometimes I get so impatient with them. Please help me to become like you. Help me to be patient.

Sometimes I get into a routine of saying my prayers and I find myself saying the same things over and over again — day after day. And then I get up and go about my daily living. Yet, instead Father, you know all of my shortcomings and you still take care of me and help me through the day. "THANK YOU LORD! THANK YOU!" Sometimes Lord I find myself all alone and Satan lets so many thoughts go through my mind. I find myself thinking about all the friends I thought that I had and all of the things that we used to do that I thought were fun. And then I cry out, "Lord please take all of these thoughts out of my mind. I don't want to ever go back to the way that I used to be and the things that we used to do!" The only time I want to think about my old friends is to tell them about the love of Christ and how much He has changed my life. And now I have that inner peace with Christ on my side and He continues to help me to be humble. Please help me to always strive to do something to help others. Help me Lord to always live my life so someone can see Christ in me. Teach me Lord to be quiet sometimes and just learn to listen for your voice.

Please Father help me to have complete faith in you and believe in you with my whole heart. I want to always depend on you like the birds in the sky and the lilies of the valley. I know that if I keep the faith you have promised me that you would do much more for me. The only thing that I have to do is to obey your word. Jesus I just want to say, "THANK YOU — for taking care of me each and every day of my life! I am not very popular and I don't possess riches or land. But Heavenly Father you looked down and found a lonely, poor forgotten sinner and you put your loving arms of protection around me and said, "This is my beloved that I have died for. If you remain faithful you will reign with me in paradise". That promise, Lord, is what keeps me going. I think sometimes about the mansions in heaven that you have prepared for us. And when I feel badly I can just imagine walking on the streets of gold or picking the sweet fruit from the tree in the middle of the garden. And, best of all, I will meet you Jesus and your Father God.

I want to thank you Lord for the inner peace that I have in serving you. Father you didn't have to choose me but you did. You gave me a chance to change my life forever and now I live for you. I want to do everything that you want me to do to lead others to you. When I am tempted the only thing I have to do is to 'CALL ON JESUS!" Satan can't stand a chance again Jesus. When I start to study your word it seems like I always get sleepy or the tape breaks. I know that it is only Satan but he can't stop me. He might slow me down for a minute, but I get right back on track. You know, Father, most of the time we sit around waiting for you to send down that great big miracle to come upon us. But we don't think of it being a miracle when we wake up each and every day, when we have food to eat, when we are on the highway so many, many times and we almost have an accident. But, Father, you sent your angels to step in and save us and we take all of these miracles for granted. When our families go out to either work or school and come home safely, "THANK YOU LORD JESUS! THANK YOU!"

I tried to put into words just how I feel about you. I know that it is not much but, in my own words, I would just like to thank you for being there for me. I know that I have a Father in heaven who I can always depend on. And I know that with Christ all things are possible. 'THANK YOU LORD!"

The Sculpture

One day many, many years ago after God finished making the world, He decided that He would make man in His own image. God bent down and first He shaped, molded and formed him so that the new man would be just right. He didn't just sit back and command that the work be done, He took His sweet time and made sure that man was perfect. He shaped man's face round and smooth; his skin was young and the color blended in perfectly. Next He put in the eyes and the color was just right. Man could see far and wide because he was given perfect vision. After that God placed his nose so that he could smell everything around him. God selected the right mouth for man and gave him the right amount of teeth so that he could be able to chew food properly. Man was given a perfect neck with a set of vocal cords you wouldn't believe so that when God met him in the beautiful garden, man could sing and talk to Him and also to the animals for hours and hours. God gave man strong arms and hands so that he could work hard, or be tender to caress the animals. God didn't have time to stop because He was not finished yet — man was only half finished.

As God continued working so enthusiastically making His man's physique flawless, then He made man the strongest set of legs on which to stand firm or run long distances and feet so strong made perfectly. When He finished molding, forming and shaping His man, he knew that He had done His best, and there was just one more thing to do. So he blew His breath into man's nostrils. This was the breath of life and man became a living soul. God place the man that He had just made into the beautiful garden. God loved him so much that everything that man could ever want was in his new home. As he walked around, he looked at everything. He named the animals, but God noticed that man didn't have a mate. So God went back to work. First He put man to sleep and took a rib from the side of him. He molded it and formed it until He had made her perfect. When man first saw her he said that she was woman. She was so beautiful. God took His time to make man and woman without any flaws. He made them so perfect nothing was left undone because He loved them so much that He wanted them to be perfect. They would never become sick. They didn't need a dentist and they didn't need a pair of glasses.

Man and woman were made by God. He named His perfect man Adam and the woman was named Eve. He put them in the beautiful garden called Eden where they roamed day and night without a care in the world. God loved them so much. He was so proud of them. After all, they were made in His image. As they walked through that beautiful garden, God told them that they could eat from any tree in the garden but one — the tree in the midst of the garden. God told them not to eat from it or even touch it or they would die. There was another being in that garden called Satan, also known as the devil. He used to be a beautiful angel in heaven until one day he decided that he wanted to be equal with God and was cast out of heaven. He took the form of a serpent, and landed in that tree in the midst of the garden.

One day as Eve walked past the tree, she heard someone talking to her. As she looked up, to her surprise, she saw a serpent and he started right away trying to convince her that God didn't really mean what He told them. He cunningly said to her, "Look, see how pretty this fruit looks. And, oh, how good it tastes". She took the fruit from the serpent and ate it. She did not die so she took the fruit to her husband and, when she finished telling him all that the serpent had told her, Adam took the fruit from her and he did eat it. So both of them had disobeyed God and they lost everything. From that moment on the world started going down and down. They saw the first death of a son committed by another son. The animals were afraid of them now.

As the years went on, the people became so wicked. They disobeyed God's laws over and over, time after time. God had forgiven them because He loved them so much. God told Noah that He wanted him to build an ark and preach to the people for one hundred and twenty years. Finally, after the end of one hundred and twenty years, God told Noah to take his family and get in the boat. God brought all of the animals on the boat and then the doors were closed. No one could get in. After that, the whole world was destroyed by the flood. After the waters had dried up Noah and his family, along with the animals, prepared to start life all over again. But soon the population had grown and the people once again disobeyed God's laws. All through the years, the people let Satan rule them and the world became weaker and more wicked because of sin.

All through the centuries you read how God's perfect man and woman have disappointed Him, time and time again You read how mankind has let Satan convince them that God didn't mean what He said in His word. Satan put all kinds of thoughts in people's minds such as, "God would never be that hard you. Just do what you want and have a nice time. He doesn't expect for you to give up your life and just act like an old person. If He wasn't God, He would be having a good time too." People all over the world listened to Satan, and they had to pay the price of sin. God sees all and He sent His only son Jesus down on this earth to help man and to teach them God's way. Satan even tried to convince Jesus that God didn't mean what He said in His word but Jesus knew what the word said and, although Satan tried to add just enough error to scripture that he quoted to Jesus that it "sounded" okay, Jesus knew the scripture and when He quoted the right way to Satan he had to turn and run because he couldn't fool Jesus. When Jesus died for our sins and was risen from the dead, we were given another chance in order to be saved. But just like Satan came to Jesus and tried to convince Him that he could give Him everything that He could ever want in life, Satan could not fool Christ because He knew all of the scriptures and He told Satan to "get behind me Satan!"

After Christ suffered and died for our sins, it seems that the world would be getting better instead of worse. But Satan knows that he has but a short time to convince the world that his way is the right way and that Christ will save the people on their terms, that they don't have to keep the commandments of God, just live their own way and God will save you. The devil tried to convince people that the Bible is the old law and we now live in the new law so you can do whatever you want. God knows your heart and He will save you anyway. But God said that He changes not. His law is forever. God gave His people a set of laws to live by many, many years ago but, through the years, people believe that they don't have to follow God's laws anymore. They feel that the law is done away with and we don't have to live by our Creator's law anymore. We have outgrown the teachings of our Father. When God looks down on us, we disappoint Him so much after all that He has done for us, even sending His only Son to die for us.

Let us examine God's laws (the Ten Commandments) now in our generation which begin in Exodus 20:2. **Commandment #1**. *The shalt have no other Gods before me (Exodus 20:3).* It seems that we have put God on the shelf although He bent down and made us in His own image. As the young people say today, we don't need to listen to God. We do our own thing. In the 1990's, everything goes. **Commandment #2.** *The shalt not make unto thee any graven image of any likeness of anything that is in heaven above or that is in the earth beneath or that is in the water under the earth. Thou shall not bow down thyself to them nor serve them for I the Lord thy God am a jealous God (Exodus 20:4,5).* In the 1990's we read the Bible and this verse means to us that in early times the people used to make golden calves or carve out their god and the people used to worship them and bring a sacrifice to it. So we figure that this doesn't concern us.

We work from sunup to sundown. We love material things so we go into debt so that we can have that huge house that we don't need and that big expensive car to sit in our big garages. This also includes every credit card in our wallets that we try to use for all the material things we desire. These things are our graven images. Anything we put before God is our image. **Commandment #3.** *Thou shalt not take the name of the Lord thy God in vain (Exodus 20:7).* But the very moment we get angry the first thing that comes out of our mouths is using God's name in vain. We are so quick to take God's name in vain but I have never heard anyone take the devil's name in vain. I have never heard anyone curse Satan, have you? People make movies about Jesus. They make pictures of Jesus. They make Him a white man with long brown hair and blue eyes, or they make Him black with an afro and brown eyes. But I have never seen a picture of the devil. I have never seen him in a picture nor have I seen him portrayed in a movie like they do Jesus.

Commandment #4. *Remember the Sabbath day to keep it holy. Six days shalt thou labor and do all thy work but the seventh day is the Sabbath of the*

Lord thy God: in it thou shalt not do any work, thou, nor thy son, nor thy daughter, thy manservant, nor thy maidservant, nor thy cattle, nor thy stranger that is within thy gates: for in six days God made heaven and earth, the sea, and all that in them is, and rested the seventh day: wherefore the Lord blessed the Sabbath day and hallowed it (Exodus 20:8-11). God gave us a rest day in the beginning. God gave us a day in which to rest from our busy week and to worship Him. But we feel that we don't have to keep the seventh day Sabbath anymore. We will give God the day that is most convenient for us. As long as we give God some of our time, that's good enough. The seventh day is our busiest day of the week. We do our shopping. We get our best bargains on the seventh day. We have to clean our houses, take the family to their games and participate in all types of outings on the seventh day.

The first day of the week is the most convenient day to serve the Lord for us. The devil has convinced us that, as long as we give God some of our time, it doesn't matter what day we serve. On the first day of the week we go to our churches and pray, sing praises to God, and after we leave church we rush out to our favorite restaurant for dinner. Then we hurry home so we can look at our favorite game on television and we feel that we have served the Lord for the week. Some stay out all Saturday night drinking, dancing and indulging in all types of drugs. They might get in about six o'clock in the morning and, no matter how drunk they are and how sleepy they are, they feel that they have to get up and go to church. The devil has the world convinced that as long as we give God some of our time, we are alright for another week.

Commandment #5. *Honor thy father and thy mother: that thy days may be long upon the land which the Lord thy God give thee (Exodus 20:12).* In Proverbs 13:24 it says, "he that spareth his rod hateth his son: but he that loveth him chasteneth him betimes". Now we don't listen to what God teaches anymore. We put the Bible on the shelf and listen to baby doctors and psychologists. Some of these professionals don't even have children and they are making a lot of money telling you how to raise your children. You don't have time to be home with your children so your children are home raising themselves. The television and their music become the babysitter. You, as parents, have no idea what your children are looking at or what they are listening to. They hang out all hours of the night and day. You have no idea who they are with or what they are doing. Your children are out of control. They have no respect for their parents. They don't care about anything with all of this going on. You still don't turn to God. Instead, you take your child to the psychologist and ask their advice.

Years ago, when your children disobeyed you, parents would discipline and teach them right from wrong. But, now, the system tells parents how not to raise their children and it is the complete opposite of the way that God in His laws tells us to raise children. It used to be a time that, when you took your children to church, they would sit on the same pew with you. Before the services started, you would take your children to the bathroom and let them get a drink of water and, in church, they were quiet during the service. Now parents go into church, sit down and their children are running wild in the other rooms of the church and you don't even think to see what that child is doing. If anyone else disciplines the child, the parent(s) gets angry. How can you discipline your child when you are in the back of the church talking and eating yourself all through the services? Children are so disrespectful now. They fight their parents, curse them, and talk to them any way they want to. Parents don't have any control over their children.

In God's law He tells children to honor their father and their mother and, because they disobey, children are killing one another. They belong to gangs. They are on drugs. Children should be happy. They should be carefree but instead they are in jails and in their graves just because they disobeyed God's law. **Commandment #6.** *Thou shalt not kill (Exodus 20:13).* When God created man and woman, He didn't mean for us to kill each other. He wanted us to love each other but, because of sin, we hate each other and now we will kill each other without blinking an eye. **Commandment #7.** *Thou shalt not commit adultery (Exodus 20:14).* When God made man and woman, He intended for them to be together forever. His desire was for us to marry one person and to make each other happy. We cannot be happy with each other because we are so busy finding fault with each other. We feel that someone else will make us happy even if it is not our mate and, before you know it, you have gone against God's law. **Commandment #8.** *Thou shalt not steal (Exodus 20:15).* People work hard in life to have nice things and, then, here comes those that won't work. They won't go to school but they will spend many hours studying how to break into your house, steal from stores or just take your purse or wallet. Most of the time these people will steal from the poor. When they go against God's law they will either end up in jail or in their graves.

Commandment #9. *Thou shalt not bear false witness against thy neighbour (Exodus 20:16).* We, as God's children, should not say things that are not true about each other. Once you start telling things that are not true it becomes easier and easier to say things that are not true, and soon people will brand you as being a liar and no one will believe you even if you are telling the truth. **Commandment #10.** *Thou shalt not covet thy neighbour's house, thou shalt not covet thy neighbor's wife, nor his manservant, nor his maidservant, nor his ox, nor his ass, nor anything that is thy neighbour's (Exodus 20:17).* We should be happy when our neighbor receives good things. Even if it seems that sometimes you can't see how good God is to you. Because we are so busy trying to see what others have, we miss our own blessings. We have to learn to be happy for others when good fortune comes to them, not be jealous and try to get what they have or try to get more. You will work yourself to death trying to "keep up with the Jones". Enjoy what you have in life because God will give you what you need. If you trust Him, you don't have to worry about what others have, you will find comfort in what you have.

God created us in His own image. He breathed the breath of life into our nostrils and we became a living soul. Because God loves us so much, he gave us His law for our guidance in life many, many years ago. The first four are the way we should love the Lord and the way we should keep His Sabbath. The last six are the way we should love and keep each other. We can live any way that we want to because that is our choice. Until we do what God wants us to do, until we learn His ways and get back to keeping His commandments, our lives will continue to go downhill. Let's get back to obeying our Creator and remember that He loves us so much that He only wants the best for us. Although we sinned against the Lord, He still loves us so much that He gave His only Son that whosoever believeth in Him should not perish, but have everlasting life (John 3:16). Here is the patience of the saints. Here are they that keep the commandments of God and have the faith of Jesus (Revelation 14:12). The commandments are found in Exodus 20:1-17. One day we will be with the Lord in Paradise.

A Very Special Friend

I had a very special friend. At first, I would only see her if we went to a family member's funeral or a picnic. I would speak and go on my way. One day she wanted to go with me to a family member's house. I really didn't want her to go with me. We really weren't very close. But after that trip, we became friends. I used to go to her home and she would tell me things about the past and stories about her life. She would just smile as she talked. I would listen to the things she shared with me. She talked about her daughter and son-in-law. She loved her five grandchildren. There wasn't anything in this world she wouldn't do for them. I got to know my very special friend as a very BEAUTIFUL ROSE. I loved her so much. I wonder if she really knew how much I loved her. I am talking about my wonderful Aunt Bert. You know how a rose springs up so beautifully and full of life? That's the way Aunt Bert was — so very full of life. Always doing things for others. She worked for years in her church and for her family.

One day she became ill. She had to go into a nursing home, but she never complained. She made the best of it. The staff loved her because she had something nice to say to them — always a nice smile when they came into her room. I have always told my family to give me my flowers while I can still smell them. I wished her church had done that. Oh it sounded nice to hear people say how good of a person that she was. But they waited until she was gone. She couldn't hear them then. I wished they could have told her face-to-face. One day after feeding the people in the park, we went by to see her. We gave her communion. We washed her feet and also her roomate's. We prayed, sang and just praised the Lord that evening. It was great, and we sang a song, "I'll Meet You in Heaven" and Aunt Bert said, "That's what I want to do, meet you in Heaven". We had such a good time. I think everyone went home happy and praising the Lord. I think all week we sang the song, "Call Him Up and Tell Him What You Want".

I went to see her whenever I could. Now I wish I would have seen her more. She loved chicken wings and White Castles and, when she had a good day, Ernie would get her some. She would eat everything on her plate. In her last days, she was sent to Jewish Hospital. From there she was sent to a hospital called Hospice. I had never heard of this hospital before. I went to see her. She had such a beautiful glow in her face. For some reason, I couldn't leave her side. I don't know if she knew that her family was there with her or not. By this time, she didn't respond to anyone. The nurses were making her as comfortable as possible. It was just a matter of time before Jesus would call His child home. But, you know — I don't care how sick a person looks, how much the doctors tell the family they give up and that they can't do anymore, the person will be right here until Jesus calls His child home.

Her granddaughter and I stayed with her the first night. The next morning, the nurse came in and told us that she would not last through the day. We called all of the family. They started coming in one by one. They stayed very late that night. Finally they all left and Rita and I went to bed. I usually can't sleep at night but, for some reason, I went right to sleep. Later on, very early in the morning about 3:00 a.m., the nurse came into the room. I jumped up, the nurse looked at me, and told me that she didn't hear a heartbeat. I sat up and looked at her. She was so still I couldn't stop looking at her. I woke Rita and told her what the nurse had told me. She said, "I knew that Momma B would just slip away". I kept looking at her. She was so still. She was at peace. I was so happy that she had been able to go to camp meeting. She wanted to see the new campground for herself. We also had a family reunion. Her granddaughter, Rita, brought her to the banquet. She looked so beautiful. I was so glad that she had a chance to take part in the things that she loved before she died.

Well, my very special friend, I have to say goodbye. No one knew the closeness we had. There were times we would talk and laugh for hours. Other times you would come over for dinner with all of my family. You were a pleasure to be around. Well, MY VERY SPECIAL FRIEND, GOODBYE UNTIL WE MEET AGAIN. That very very beautiful, beautiful ROSE has come to full bloom and has withered and died. But, one day soon, Jesus will wake His child up and she will be all in full bloom again.

GOODBYE MY VERY, VERY SPECIAL FRIEND.

Be Kind to Your Fellow Man

Someone made this statement once, "Be kind to the people you meet going up the ladder of success because you will meet these same people when you are on your way back down". I laughed when I heard it, but oh how true that statement is. Have you ever noticed how small children treat one another? They are much different than adults. When children meet each other they really show that they care about one another. They don't care whether or not they are black or white, oriental or Indian, tall or short. They don't focus on whether their hair is a different color or different texture. And they have the cutest set of eyes you have ever seen — some large, some small, some slanted, all different colors. But small children don't care. When they look into each others' eyes, they only see this small person just like themselves — someone they can share their food and toys with, hug and kiss, or just play with. But as they get older, adults teach children to be prejudiced and to hate. That's when children start being cruel to other children — making fun of the way others look, their color, size, and even the texture of their hair. We make fun of others just because the person is different.

As we start to climb the ladder of success and grow older, we meet all sorts of people in our everyday life. Some we treat any kind of way, and will say anything we want to them. We learn how to "wheel and deal" at a very early age so we tend to find people who are weak. They really believe you are their friend, or that you are there to really give them the help that they need. You know how to get their confidence. You make them feel that you have their best interest at heart. Then you use them any way you want to. Finally they find you out and know you for what you really are, and start to tell other people how you have belittled them and made them feel like they are nothing. And when you discover that people know about you, then you start putting that person "down" — making all types of false statements about them. You create all kinds of excuses to make yourself look good because you have the clout. And you know the right people to help you get out of messes that you get yourself into. The person feels that the whole thing is their fault. The person is no longer in your life and you move on.

After a while it becomes a habit. You learn to use people over and over until you think that you can do whatever you want to and get away with it — because you have always come out on top. Sooner or later the person will leave. After a while no one will even remember just what happened and you just keep on climbing on up that ladder to success. BUT GOD IS STILL ON THE THRONE! He sees and hears all. Sometimes He lets you run on like there is no tomorrow. But, eventually, you have to start that climb back down that ladder. You are no longer associated with the right people. You see, God stepped in and everything is out in the open. You no longer can lie and cheat people like you used to. You can no longer call on someone in high places to bail you out. You have now fallen all the way down the ladder. Who is there to pick you up? Believe it or not — the same people you used, you deceived, and lied on are there and are still willing to help you — even now. These are the Lord's children and He gives them a forgiving heart.

Sometimes the Lord has to let you fall all the way down the ladder before He can help you. Because sometimes when you are successful you tend to forget about the Lord — until you get into trouble. And, only then, do you realize how much you need the Lord. Now you need to find the Lord all over again in your life. Now you think about all the wrong things you have done through the years, and how badly you have treated your Heavenly Father and your fellow man. As you think about all that has happened in your life and all the trouble you have brought upon yourself,

DO YOU THINK THE CLIMB UP THE LADDER WAS WORTH IT?
DO YOU!?

Prodigal Son

Remember, my little children, the story of the Prodigal Son — how he longed for something better, something different from what the father had for him. We know that this is a story that Jesus taught to the people. All of us, at one time or another, wanted to get out "into the world". We wanted to have fun. We thought we had too much living to do. We have no time for Jesus right now. We will wait until we are older. That's the way the Prodigal Son was. He felt that there was something out there that he had not experienced, places he hadn't seen. His father was very wealthy so he asked him for his share of the wealth. He took his share of the wealth, hugged his father and brother and left his home to go to a distant land. He was so happy. He had so many friends. They had a party every night and he paid for everything. Women crowded around him, men brought him everything that he wanted. He thought that he was a king. They danced. They drank the best wine. They had a big gambling game going every night. Oh what a good time he was having! He was so glad that he had left his father's house. This was the life. He was never going home again.

Satan always makes us feel that we are having a very good time. When we are in the world, we are playing in the devil's playfield and, when we follow the devil, we always end up in trouble. The Prodigal Son went on from day to day acting as though there was no tomorrow. His father watched and waited everyday for his son to come home. The son was having such a good time with his new friends he forgot all about his father and his home. He planned to make this strange land his new home. But one day famine hit this strange land and all of his money was gone. He found himself alone, hungry and with no place to stay. All of his so-called friends left him. After all of the money and good times he showed them, they couldn't even give him a meal or a place to stay. So he just roamed the streets, day and night, so weak from hunger and no sleep he finally took a job caring for the swine. And, as he was eating with the pigs, he remembered he had a father whose servants were living and eating better than he was.

Sometimes we have to reach "rock bottom" before we remember we have a Savior, who is waiting patiently for us to call upon Him. So he decided to go home to his father. He had planned to ask his forgiveness and to further ask him if he could just be a servant. Every day since he left, his father waited and longed for his son to come home. One day, as he stood waiting and watching, he saw someone coming down the road. As he watched, he realized that it was his son. Just as the son started to ask the father if he could be a servant of his, the father grabbed him and called for the servant to bring his robe and ring for his son. Everyone rejoiced because that which was lost finally came home. Our Heavenly Father is so good to us. He blesses us each and every day of our lives.

The holy spirit is pleading to us trying to get us to change our lives before it is too late. Please come back to Him before it's to late. Patiently and tenderly Jesus is waiting for you and for me. If Jesus wanted to, He could make us serve him. He could threaten us. He could yank us back by the neck, shake us until we come to our senses. But Jesus doesn't try to make us serve Him. We are given a choice to make our own decision whether to follow Him all the way or you don't have to — it's your choice. Jesus loves all of us, and it saddens Him when we decide to turn our backs on Him.

Let God cover us with His whole armor of protection. That's the only protection you have against Satan's trickery. Jesus did not die because of the Roman soldier's spear. He did not die because of the nails in His hands and feet. He did not die because of the extreme agony of the cross. He did not die from a loss of blood. Jesus died when His Father withdrew His life-giving presence from Him — thus showing us just how deadly it is to be separate from God (Matt. 27:46, Mark 15:34).

Thirty Pieces of Silver

If the Lord would ask you today what He could grant you to make you happy, what would you ask for? Well — would it be long life, a good companion, beautiful obedient children, enough money to live comfortably, a nice home, a new car, or good health and plenty of food? The Lord might say, "Okay, you will have what you asked for". Do you think that would make us happy? Sometimes I might have cookies, cake or some candy in the house. But, at that moment, I don't want what I have there. I am trying to get to the store to buy some ice cream. Why? Because we are never satisfied. Some might have a nice home, a good job, and doing good in life. You feel happy for a while but, one day, your neighbor or a family member might drive up in a brand new car or purchase a new home. You can't stand it! You forget about all of the nice things that you have and start scheming and cheating trying to outdo the next person. We are never satisfied with what we have.

Jesus chose 12 men. These 12 men came from ALL walks of life, but Jesus brought them together and made them His Disciples. He loved them so much. He taught them about the love of God, His Father. He performed miracle after miracle. He healed the sick and raised the dead. He taught the people in parables but this is not how He instructed His Disciples. He taught them everything they needed to know. They saw Jesus feed the people twice, and the Disciples collected 12 baskets. One time, after feeding over 5,000 people and after feeding over 4,000, the Disciples were there. Jesus taught them the Lord's Prayer. He knew that they had to continue on after he had to leave. So he taught them EVERYTHING.

The last time the Disciples were alone with Jesus was in the Upper Room. Jesus was still trying to teach them to be humble. He wrapped a towel around Himself, bent down and washed all of the Disciples feet. The Lord loved them with all of His heart, and He felt so sorry for them that they didn't understand what He was trying to teach them. He knew that they could not stand when His time was over — and He HAD to leave them. The only thing that they had in mind was being the highest in Christ's kingdom. Their minds were not on the miracles that He performed day after day. They didn't have their minds on helping Jesus — only trying to please Him so He would pick them to be the greatest when he started His kingdom.

Like so many of us, we can't see that we have everything that we need. We are always looking for more. The Disciples had Jesus walking in their midst, and they wanted more! What more could they have wanted? They had THE BEST! Our Heavenly Father had chosen them to be His Disciples. When it was time for the life of Jesus to end, He still tried to protect and take care of his Disciples. He asked them to pray to His Father for strength. Instead of praying, they went to sleep. When the Disciples saw the soldiers, they ran away. Peter stayed nearby, but he denied Jesus three times. Judas, who also walked with Jesus, had his mind focused on money and fame so he let Satan come into his life and convince him to betray Jesus for 30 pieces of silver — the price of a slave. At the end, Judas found out that he didn't need the money. he didn't even want it, but it was too late.

No one knows why Judas did what he did to Jesus. Jesus should have been born into this world as royalty with servants waiting on Him hand-and-foot. He was born poorly. He was born to a virgin in the stable, laid in a manger, and wrapped in swaddling clothes. His Heavenly Father never forgot Him because, at His birth, a star appeared in the sky where the shepherds tended their sheep. They followed the star to where the baby laid and brought Him gifts. At that moment, Jesus was treated as royalty. When Jesus started His Ministry He knew that He had to go through deep, deep agony — that He would not be accepted as the son of God. He loved us and He knew that He was THE ONLY CHANCE that we had TO BE SAVED. Jesus prayed to His Father all the time. He only wanted to do the will of His Father. Even in His final hour, the only thing He wanted was to see His Father's face.

After Jesus died and was resurrected, the people realized who Jesus was. They knew that He was the Son of God. Although we had treated Jesus very badly, He still met with His Disciples to send them the Holy Spirit to be a Comforter so they would not be alone when He had to leave them. His mind must have been on all of the pain and suffering that He was about to endure, but He took the time to focus on His Disciples who He knew would be lost without Him when He left. What a wonderful Savior we serve — to love us so much that He gave His life TO SAVE US ALL! We can point fingers, and ask the question, why? How could the Disciples turn against Jesus the way that they did? As close as He was to Peter, regardless of how scared Peter was, it seems that Peter should have been there for Jesus. But he denied Him — not once, but three times. The other Disciples ran away, all except Judas. He SOLD Jesus out for 30 pieces of silver! Now, that's all 12 of them. How do we think that they rated as followers of Jesus?

We would probably say, "I would never treat Jesus that way, I love Him too much! I would do anything for Him!" We are so busy that we don't have time to spend with Him and, when we do settle down and start to study, we go to sleep. We keep our minds so filled with so many other things that we cannot hear what the Holy Spirit has to tell us. Isn't that what happened to the Disciples? We have the Disciples as an example. Instead of criticizing the Disciples, we need to learn from them. Learn how Jesus loved them — just like He loves us. Read how Jesus took them aside and taught them, showing them how they should have faith. They only had to have enough faith as a little mustard seed. If you show a LITTLE faith, you would be surprised what you can do (Luke 17:5-6). The Holy

Spirit is warning us and has been doing so from generation to generation — telling us that the end is near. We see it each and every day. Our people have become so violent. No one cares about killing each other. Drugs are everywhere. Parents are against children and children are against parents. There is no love anywhere. We are being warned every day of our lives.

The world is not getting better, it is getting worse. Don't let the time come and we are not prepared — just like the Disciples were not ready when Jesus' time came. They didn't know what to do because they were not listening to what Jesus was trying to teach them. They had a second chance and they finally understood what Jesus was trying to teach them. Let's stop pointing the finger or asking pointless questions and do what the Lord tells us. The signs are all around us. Tell others how much the Lord loves them and that He has gone to prepare us a mansion. Let's be ready when our time comes. Study and learn from others' mistakes in the Bible so that you will be strong and ready WHEN JESUS COMES BACK TO CLAIM HIS OWN.

Take the Time to Say Thank You

How many times in your busy life have you taken the time out just to tell someone, "Thank you" or "I love you"? We really mean to but we get busy and forget. One day my son and I were driving along and talking and, in the conversation he said, "I just want to thank you Mom for being a mother to me. It kind of brought tears to my eyes. I felt good inside. When you become a parent, you are not given instructions on how to raise that little person who is put into your arms. You just have to do the best you can — and some of your children need a little more care than others. They have their own personality. No two children are alike. But you have to let them know that you are there for them, and that you will always love them. Not only children but parents should tell their children sometimes that you love them. I think that everyone wants to hear someone say, "You really did a good job" or "I really love you".

Last year I received my first plaque. I was so happy because you feel sometimes that no one cares and when someone does something nice for you it makes you feel that someone loves you. You don't go around telling everyone what you do, but when someone recognizes things that you do it really makes you feel like going on. It's a shame that people only tell the good things that you have done after you are gone. At that time, your family hears all of the good things that you have done in your life. So many times you have worked long hours at the church doing all kinds of jobs. When you are gone, your pastor speaks so highly of you — how kind you were to others and how you spent hours helping someone in need. Some things maybe you had forgotten yourself. Even you family members remember things that you did for them. Some things they hadn't thought of in years and wish they had told you themselves.

As they sit around telling story after story, remembering what kind of person that you were, they miss you. They know that no one could ever take your place. I don't care how great everyone speaks about your loved one or how long each person talks, they are not speaking to the person — but their families. Because, when you are gone, you can't hear any of those good things and you can't see all of the good things that are being done for you. Your family can say that they really thought a lot about her or him but, after everything is over, no one will remember.

There was a family that I knew. They used to always hug each other. They would do it unconsciously. They would see one another and would hug and kiss each other, smile, and say "I love you". How sad because they didn't mean it! They wanted the neighbors to think that they were the ideal family. But behind closed doors, the love was not there. There were no hugs and kisses. Too many of our families are this way. We never have a kind word to say to each other. We take each other's love for granted. We think that person will be here forever.

I have heard some people years after their loved one had passed, telling anyone who would listen how good that person was, and how much that person did for you. Everyone around you listened. Some get tired of hearing that story, but the one who should have heard about how much you love and need them is gone. They will never hear about how much you needed them in life because you never took the time to tell them. You just took it for granted that they knew how you felt about them.

Remember, when a person is good to you in life and will stand by you through thick and thin, you really have a special friend. And in our churches when we have faithful members who love the Lord with all of their hearts and will do all that they can to do the will of the Lord, we must appreciate them. Sometimes we outgrow the person's love and we forget all of the good things that they did for us. We really forget that because of that person's worrying, crying, and much prayers you are the person that you are today! You could never have done it on your own and, even in our churches, there are members who have been our strength. Remember them sometimes because, without the hard work and long hours, the churches could not be run as smoothly as they are today. Don't just forget about them until it is too late. Tell the person how much you love them and how much you appreciate all that they have done for you. Remember, the Lord sees all and knows all — even if the person is never recognized.

JESUS WILL COME BACK ONE DAY AND
HE WILL HAVE HIS REWARDS WITH HIM!

The Forgotten Generation

One day there was a beautiful little boy or girl whose life started many, many years ago. They had their lives all planned out. They worked very, very hard all of their lives. They made mistakes but they taught us to do better and, we learned from their mistakes. For many years they had to take a lot of abuse from other races. They were degraded, put down, and belittled for our sakes. A lot of them were never educated because they had to work in the fields. They had to take care of other people's children while their own children went neglected. Some went on to educate themselves, and some went on to help others in their search for life. But, as the next generations were born (their children, grandchildren and great, great grandchildren), these older members made sure that the new generations had much more in life than the older generation could ever know. So the younger generation knows more because the older generation made sure that they had a better life. They were given the best education they could get. They were given the most expensive homes, the latest clothes. Some never knew what bad times were all about. They never had to be degraded by other races. Although sometimes, even now, it seems that they are still not on the same level as other races. It is nothing like it was years ago.

In some cultures our senior citizens are respected and honored. But in our society we do not give our older members the respect that they deserve. They try to give us advice and share with us some of their many memories. But we half-listen to them because they don't know what they are talking about. They just keep talking and talking and sometimes you don't understand what they are saying. But do listen. Just because their hair is white now and they can't get around like they used to anymore, they still have a lot of wisdom. And we can always learn a very important lesson from them. Now the seniors are very old and they feel so all alone. They have no one to tell their experiences to. All of their friends and family are gone now. The world has changed right in front of them. They have no one to turn to. They have no one to tell their experiences to anymore. Oh what a loss because our youth could learn so much about the trials and tribulations our older generations have gone through. If our children have the time to listen to them, maybe there would not be so much disrespect.

Children do not respect their elders because they haven't been taught to. Parents are so busy working and planning their lives trying to give their children a better life. They are so tired that they don't have the time to raise their children. So, a lot of times, the children are on their own. It would be so nice if our youth could become friends with an older person, help them and just get to know them. But, instead, no one seems to remember the older person. They stay all alone in their houses. No one comes to visit. No one thinks to call anymore. No one cares about them. They have worked all of their lives. Now that they are too old and too weak to work, they just sit in a chair all day — day in and day out. The days seem to get longer and the nights seem to last forever until they get so feeble they are no longer able to care for themselves. So they are put in a nursing home. That is their last stop. When they reach the home, it is as though they were already dead. They sit in their rooms day after day with only the staff to talk to when they come into the room to take care of the person.

Every now and then the member of the older generation may be picked up for church and maybe they might have a visitor. Sometimes their birthday might be remembered and have flowers sent to them. There they stay until they die. One thing the younger generation forgets is that it was the older person who helped to build our churches. They were there when changes were made. They paid their tithes for many, many years. It was the older person who did the cleaning of the churches, did all of the cooking when there were guests in the church. They visited the sick and gave the best wisdom that they could give. But now they are old and forgotten. They can't see well anymore. They can't walk anymore. But they still have their memories. No one can ever take that away from them. They used to be full of energy and strength, living their lives to the fullness — but now,

THEY ARE THE FORGOTTEN GENERATION!

Have You Tried It?

This question was asked of us as we were busy sitting around talking about that elderly person who had to be put in the nursing home because she had no one to take care of her. We were trying to figure out who we could get to go out and visit her, or who would take her back and forth to church. One person suggested that she was so old, she didn't really know that she was at church anyway. It was too much trouble going and picking her up each week for her to sit up and sleep through the whole service. The others agreed. No one wanted to take the time with her. Everyone was too busy with their families and jobs. Another one said that they just didn't have the patience to be bothered with her.

As we went back and forth about who would be responsible for this poor elderly person who is now all alone, a hand went up in the back of the room and a very attractive gentleman stood up. He looked at us all before he spoke. Then he said, "Please forgive me for interrupting, but may I ask you all a question"? No one said a word, we just listened. He continued, "I have heard everyone voice their opinion about this dear soul who has lived her whole life loving the Lord and working in the church. I would like to know how many of you would trade places with her? How many would step into her shoes? At one time she had a mother, father, sister and brother. One by one they have all passed away. There was a time that she was like all of you. Some of you are blessed with a husband or wife with children and grandchildren. "Praise the Lord!"

What I would like for you to do is to close your eyes for a little while, will you? Let's say you are this little lonely lady. Now all of you here might have aches and pains, but you can get around. This lady can't walk anymore. Can you imagine never walking again? All she does all day is sit in a wheelchair or lay down in the bed. When you go home and close the door, your family is around you and you are not alone. So no one could ever imagine what it would be like to be all alone in this world. What if her family becomes yours? Now you have a father, mother, sister, and brothers. Let's say this is a typical night at home with your family. You can see your mother preparing the family meal. You can just hear her humming her favorite hymn as she rushes around in her kitchen stirring the pots, checking the bread. Oh boy, you can almost smell the aromas. You and your sister are setting the table. Everything has to be just right.

Just as you finish, the door opens and father comes in from work. After he greets the family, he goes in to wash up for dinner. Your brothers are upstairs and they come down when they hear their father's voice. Mother calls, "Dinner is ready!" and the whole family joins in the dining room for the evening meal. Father offers the blessing. You all say your favorite Bible verses. How do you feel? Don't you feel happy right now sitting around the table eating and discussing the events of the day with your family. You feel surrounded by love.

That's what love is all about — LOVE. After dinner everyone goes into the living room to study their lessons and sing the praises to the Lord, and you all join hands to pray thanking God for allowing us to come together just one more time. How wonderful you must feel knowing your family is close. This makes you feel kind of snug, kind of safe, kind of important — doesn't it?

But, wait! Open your eyes! Who do you see? No one is here! Everyone is gone! They didn't leave all at once, but one by one. First your father passes. Finally you get used to losing your father, then your mother passes. You lose one brother, then the other brother. Now it's just you and a sister. There is no need to have those big meals anymore. It's just the two of you, but you still have someone with you. Then one day God saw fit to take the last member of your family. Now you have no one — no one!" You are the only one left. At this point the gentleman pauses. He asked a question. How many of you are all alone? After you have put yourself in this person's place and you have lost your whole family, tell me how do you feel? Please raise your hand and tell me how it feels to be all alone. No one raised their hand. No one spoke a word. He waited a few minutes before he continued to speak.

He reminded them of the story of Lazarus and the rich man. Let's say that Lazarus was not only the poor beggar but he could have been that poor old lady in the nursing home who needed someone just to reach out to them. Time after time when you see that old person at church you may speak and introduce yourself to them. Some may even hug them. And then you walk right by them and go home. The rich man might not only be rich money-wise but he could be you, healthy enough to get around, having a nice car, good food to eat and a nice family all around you. And because you spend five or ten minutes with this person you have done your Christian duty.

If Jesus was walking on this earth, He would just reach down and take her by the hand be her family. He would lift her up and she would be like new again. With Jesus on her side she wouldn't need any of you. Jesus would tell her, "Come on up sister or brother, you have been faithful over a few things. I will make you ruler over many". But the rich man will be somewhere watching this poor soul who now has everything. Now the rich man is begging for Lazarus to help him. He now has nothing. Read Luke 16:19-25. He went on to say, "We preach love, we pray love, and we even teach love. But when we are confronted with love how do we act"? Before you answer, just try walking a mile in someone else's shoes!".

After the man finished speaking we just looked at each other. We thought about what he had said and started making plans for doing better. We started testifying to how good God has been to us. How He has taken care of us all of these years. And we want Jesus to say to us one day, "I was hungry or sick and you fed me and visited me" And you say, "When did I see you hungry or sick and I fed you or visited you"? And He says unto me, "inasmuch as you have done it unto one of the least of these my brethren ye have done it unto me" (Matt. 25:34-40). We felt badly for the way that we had acted and what was worse of all, a stranger had to bring it to our attention. We turned to say, "Thank God for sending him to us". And to our surprise, he was gone. No one saw him come in and no one saw him leave.

God's Smallest Miracle

I witnessed a very small miracle on November 26, 1991. I would never have believed it if I hadn't seen it for myself. My son called me early that Monday to tell me that their baby was not going to make it. His wife had to be rushed to the hospital. Her water had "broken". There wasn't any warning — it just happened. Although the baby did not come right away, the doctor didn't do anything to help the baby because he was too young. You see, he was only 19 weeks old and his lungs had not developed yet. If he had been 20 or 23 weeks old, they could have saved him — so they did nothing to help this little guy. So. about 7:20 a.m. on that Tuesday morning, my son called me to tell me the baby was born and it was a boy. But he kept saying, "Mom he is so little, what shall I do with him? Shall we bury him? How can we? He is just too little". I had no idea what he was talking about. I understood that he was small, but I thought he was the size of a small baby.

When I arrived at the hospital with my sister at 2:30 p.m., the baby was no longer in the room. I was kind of relieved because I didn't really know how I would react to seeing the baby. My sister and I talked about it on the way to the hospital. My daughter was already in the room with the parents. I asked her if she had held the baby and she told me no, but the father had held him most of the day. The mother said that she looked at him and held him a little while. But the father took his little baby in his arms and just held him. They knew that they would have him for just a little while.

When we arrived, the baby was not in the room. About two hours later the father wanted to baptize his infant son. As we waited for the nurse to bring the baby to the room I felt kind of funny — like mixed emotions. Did I want to see him or not? As I thought about it, there was a knock at the door and a nurse came in with a little bundle in her arms. She laid the blanket down and left the room. We all gathered around as the father opened the blanket. At first I peeped. So did my sister and my daughters but, then, the blanket was fully opened and there laid this little human being, not as big as the palm of your hand. So tiny, so beautiful. Who would ever believe that this was once a living being. A very small person that had a heartbeat.

As I looked into the blanket, I saw a little head about the size of a small ball. He was fully developed with his eyes, nose, ears even eyebrows. He looked like a little toy doll. He had little tiny arms with the most perfect little hands and all of his fingers. His body was formed and the smallest legs, ten little toes, and the smallest feet you have ever seen. On November 26, 1991 the father, mother, grandmother and three aunts witnessed a very little miracle — a miracle that only God could have made. Man, in all his wisdom, could never make something so perfect as this baby. Until this little angel came into our lives, I had no idea that a baby of 19 weeks would be so developed — so perfect, so very small. As we all joined together singing and listening to a Bible text while the baby was being baptized, I think we all had tears in our eyes. We knew that would be the last time we could see the little human being. My son handed the baby to me. I held him in my arms. My thoughts at that time were to just hold him tight. His little sister thought he was a little toy. His mother just looked on.

My son told us that, although he felt sad about loosing his little son, he knew that when we put our trust in God He helps us to find peace in Him. Because we have Christ in our lives, He will help us find pleasure even in bad times. So they found pleasure for a little while. Once we learn to trust in the Lord He will lead you through all things good or bad. Only trust Him. He has promised to help you. These parents had a little son prematurely. They will never hear him cry. They will never be able to do all the things we take for granted day by day for our children. But we are so busy worrying about the child's color or texture of the child's hair (which doesn't mean a thing). The only thing that should matter is that our children are healthy. Take time with your children. Love them and teach them about the Lord. You know they are only on loan to us anyway. After the baby was baptized, the father wrapped him back up and said to him, "Goodbye, son, I'll see you in Heaven".

A Portrait of a Family

Once upon a time there was a family. They were so beautiful together. They were like looking at a portrait to others. People would see them and say, "I wish my family was as close as yours". This family was so good to one another. they would do everything together. If you would see one, you would see them all. Soon the family was not as close as they used to be. They didn't have that "family portrait look" anymore. They were no longer that special family who people used to see and admire. Some of the members were still close and when others became ill, they would see about them. Some were sick, with illnesses that could kill them at any time if the sickness was not controlled by medicine. The ones who were still close rallied around the sick ones. They did everything that they could for the sick members of the family, helping them with whatever they needed. But God still blessed them. They started to get better after many, many prayers. They started having good things happen in their lives. So, one by one, they started fighting about crazy things. They acted very childish about material things that will be here today and maybe gone tomorrow.

This beautiful family started arguing and even cussing each other out and never once said that they were sorry. They stopped speaking to members of their families for years, and I bet if you asked them what they were arguing about they didn't even know. All families have arguments. That's life! But only someone who doesn't have good sense would fall out with a person and never pick up a phone or go to their house and talk to them. I don't care what went down, they are there with you through sickness and even through major surgery. It is only by the grace of God that you came through the surgery, and you prayed to God that He would bring you through it. But you went to the hospital without getting things right with you loved ones. The illness that you have might lead to a heart attack and kill you. Are you ready to meet your Maker? Time and time again you ask God to have mercy on you and you ask God to forgive you. How do you think that God will forgive you when you can't forgive your loved one?

Do you know that life is not promised to you. The day is not promised to you! Even though you woke up today how do you know that you will even live through the day? Or how do you know that family members will live through the day? Remember, this person has been so good to you, and you always said how much you loved them. You will never forget them. How does this family think that God is going to keep blessing them when nothing changes? When your time comes to die and, keep in mind, no one knows when his or her time is up — will you have time to call or visit that loved one? How can you forget what a person has done for you in life? One thing is certain, God saw what that person did for you and He will reward them for it.

I would like to share a couple of stories with you. These two sisters just couldn't get along. They argued every time they were together, so they decided to stay apart. But their mother's dream was that these two sisters would love each other. She just wanted them to get along. She planned a picnic and all the children came and brought the grandchildren with them. Everything was going fine. But the mom was on "pins and needles" hoping no one said the wrong thing to get these two started. When the parents can't get along, how do you think that the children will get along? That's what had happened. The grandchildren "passed" some words and, because one sister didn't discipline her child, they started arguing and cussing. They wanted to fight each other. They ended up saying such nasty things, telling each other that they hated one another and hoped that the other one was dead. Then they grabbed their things and children and left — never seeing each other again alive. One sister had a heart attack during the night and died. When the other sister heard about her sister's death, the only thing that she could do was to scream and yell — saying over and over how much she loved her sister and asking her to forgive her. But she couldn't hear her. It was too late. The sister who was left almost lost her mind. The mother told her, "Don't worry, she really knows that you loved her". But, did she? The only way she would have known that the one sister loved the other was by her actions. The way she treated her sister and the way she talked to her sent a very painful message. What are we showing our children? How can we show them that we love them when we can't love each other?

My second story is about this family that was going to attend their family reunion. Two sisters were on the phone making arrangements on the time that they should leave. They decided to leave at 6:00 a.m. The next morning, the one sister arrived at the other sister's house and let herself in. She called her sister and didn't get an answer. All of the lights were on and the bed was made. The one sister called and called, then she walked around to the other side of the bed. She wondered where her sister could have been that early in the morning. At that moment, she found her sister on the floor. As the one sister bent down to see if her sister was alive, she called 911 who pronounced her sister dead. She never would have thought that when she arrived to pick her sister up to attend their family reunion that she would find her sister dead.

Listen families, life is not promised to us! When we are born or when we die, ONLY God knows how long we will live or when it is time for us to die. WE HAVE TO LOVE ONE ANOTHER AND LEARN TO FORGIVE ONE ANOTHER. Don't stay angry with each other for months and sometimes years about things that wouldn't mean a thing if something would happen to one of you.

While I was typing this paper I was listening to a program on television. It was the life story of Patti LaBelle. Patti was remembering her life with her younger sister, Jackie. She said that she and Jackie used to have fights with each other and just kind of stayed away from each other. One day Jackie told Patti that she had cancer, and she was taking treatments for her cancer. Patti said she told Jackie, "Keep on taking your treatments, you will be around for a long time". They didn't talk much after that. Patti really did love her sister, but she just never told her. One day Patti woke up and said, "I'm going to see my sister and I'm going to tell her how much I really do love her and from now on we will be close". As Patti was walking out of the door, she stopped to answer the phone. The person on the other end told her that just a short time ago her sister had passed away — she was gone. Patti never had a chance to tell her sister how she felt about her. How sad that she didn't get a chance to see her sister before she died. And the next time she will see her sister, she will be just a "shell" of her sister. She can't talk to her sister anymore. She will not see her again until Jesus comes again.

The reason I am sharing these stories with you is to let families know that they should love one another. How can you teach your children to love each other when you don't even know how to love your own loved ones? Each one of these stories that I have included in this letter was true. God has given you a chance to make things right in your life. How many chances do you think you are going to get? All families at some time or another will have a disagreement. That's natural. But what's not natural is that you have an argument with a family member and you stay angry for years — not speaking to your loved ones or their children. When you get angry with one of your loved ones, you tend to treat their children as though they were strangers. You don't know what's going on in their lives and you dont' even care. Remember when you walk around thinking you are better than this child that you are, in fact, no better than they are because they are part of you — because you are family. You can give your loved one a hug and show them that you care. Sometimes they get on your nerves, but they are your loved ones and you are stuck with them.

When you look at a portrait of a family everyone looks so beautiful, as they smile for the picture. One thing that is certain is that as you look at this family portrait, they all look alike. As you look from face to face, you can see that they all belong to the same family. And, if you think that your loved one is no good, well then you must not be any good because they are part of you. Take time out to love your loved ones. Don't wait until it is too late for you to be a part of their lives. DO IT NOW! Go back and look at one of your family portraits. Look at each one's face. They smile so beautifully. Anyone looking at a picture of your loved ones will think that you are the most loving family in the world. Take time now! Don't put it off any longer!

Become the loving family that you know you can be!

Were You There?

Were you there when Jesus was born into this world, poor with no place to lay His head? Were you there when He was baptized and His Father in Heaven was well-pleased? Were you there when the devil tempted our Lord for 40 days and 40 nights? Even though He was without food and water, He didn't give up. He passed the test. Were you there when Jesus selected His Disciples and they walked with Him each and every day and saw Him work miracle after miracle healing the sick, raising the dead, feeding the hungry, casting out devils, making the lame to walk and the deaf to hear. Oh what a mighty God we serve. NO! You were not there when Jesus bled and died on the cross to save our souls. NO! We were not there when Jesus walked this earth. You have read about the life of Christ many times in the Bible and you might say to yourself, Oh Jesus was wonderful.

You are so impressed with Jesus and the way He helped the people — ALL THE PEOPLE! And it didn't make a difference what color your skin was or whether you were male or female. The only thing Jesus had to know was that the person needed help. No one has ever seen the face of Our Lord, but every time you look into the face of that homeless person living on the street needing someone to give them a meal or money to help with a place to stay, you can imagine Jesus' face. What about that mother who has small children and is trying to raise them all by herself who needs someone to reach out and give her a hand with them or take time out to just talk to her. And then there is that young child wanting to join a gang because he feels that he is not loved at home, and he feels that the gang members will be his friends. Talk to him, show him that gangs don't help people and that they hurt people.

Show the young child that there is a man named Jesus who loves him, and wants him to go home. Help him and his family to study and pray together, to get their lives together.

And we must not forget that young teenager who wants a baby so that she can have someone to love. Show that young teenager that that is not a reason to bring a baby into the world. She is too young to become a mother. Share with her that she has her whole life ahead of her. Spend time with her and NEVER put her down. Show her the love of God. It just might change her life. We must NEVER FORGET that older person who might need someone to go to the store, pay bills, or cook a meal. When you walk down the street and see that person with a needle in his arm trying to get high, what do you do? When you pass that woman standing on the corner trying to make a dollar, what do you do? And when you see that old friend of yours killing themselves with alcohol and cigarettes, what can you do? Can you help? Just ask yourself what would Jesus do?

Every time you look into the face of that young child hoping to find love in a gang, that teenage girl trying to find someone to love, feel the compassion of Jesus and REACH OUT! Let everyone you meet in this world know that nobody has even seen the face of God but, when you see the face of the people around you regardless of who they are or how they look, help them because THAT'S WHAT JESUS WOULD DO. Remember, when you look at people around you, you are looking at the face of God!

I'm Grown!

One day I heard a group of young people talking. One of them said to the other, "Man, I can't wait until I am grown. When I am grown I can do whatever I want to, stay out as long as I please, and my parents can't tell me nothing. If they do, I'll just look at them and tell them I'm grown now I can do whatever I want to!" I have been watching our young people. They want to be grown so that they can stay out in the streets all night and sleep all day. Now what could they be doing that it would take all night to finish? They have too much idle time on their hands, and that idle time becomes the devil's workshop. Because at night our young people hang out on the corners, finding all the wrong things to do — like stealing and having unprotected sex with anyone who is willing. The drug dealer is also hanging around on the corner looking for you so he can make his money. Our young people are engaged in fighting and killing, and one thing you must realize is that it only takes one time to kill someone, get busted with drugs, or steal and get arrested. Then what do you grown people do when you are no longer in juvenile courts?

Now you end up in the penitentiary or the cemetery. The first time you so-called grown people get arrested, you call your Mom crying to her to help you. Now, you don't understand what it means to be grown. Being grown means accepting responsibility for your life, having your own place to live, buying your own food and clothes, and having your own transportation. Young people, all of this means you must have a job. It means you listen to your parents and show them respect. After all they have been grown a lot longer than you have, and they can tell you all the knocks and bumps that they have already gone through. Because you are grown, that doesn't mean you can stand on the corner and holler at your "homey's". That's not what makes you grown. And then run to Mom's house whenever you get into trouble. After a while, begging from family members to family members doesn't work.

Young people, if you want to be grown and get ahead, stay in school and get the best education you can so that you can get the best jobs. That's the only way that you can survive in life. You need to select better friends. Sometimes the ones that you think are your friends, are not. They might get jealous because you may have a closer relationship with your family and your friends might not have the same relationship with their family. So they try to turn you against them — telling you that your parents are too strict on you and you need to stop listening to them. Or because you are close to graduation and your friends have already dropped out of school and have no future, they may try to influence you to drop out by saying that you will never make it. Young people, they are not your friends. They don't care about you. The only thing they want you to do is to fail. You have to use your own mind and think for yourself.

Remember who your real friends are. They are your family members. Your Mom has always been on your side. You can always count on her. Even when you are at your worse. But she's the first one who you will turn on. Sometimes you will curse at her. You might even fight her, but she is always there for you. Our young people think the world owes them something. But people, the world owes you nothing. If you just sit around all day and don't help yourself, nobody is going to do it for you. Young people, learn to take care of yourself by living the best that you can. You might think that you are too young to learn about Christ right now. But you're not! You are at the right age to carry God's word to all who will listen. Can't you see how the rap music persuades young people to do whatever the music tells them to do? Well, if you give your life to the Lord, you can turn not only your life around but also your friends. Instead of them influencing you to do the wrong thing, you can influence them to learn about the Lord — to turn not only their lives around but yours. There is one verse that I know you can take with you anywhere, and it can help you always:

I CAN DO ALL THINGS THROUGH CHRIST WHICH STRENGTHEN ME
(Phil. 4:13).

The Contest

As I watched the Mr. Universe Contest last night, I know that it was all in fun but when I was driving home, I started thinking about the love that Christ has for us verses the contests of life. Let's talk about Christ's love for us. No one ever loved us so much that they would be willing to die for us. Who would ever think about us like Christ does? He understands and forgives us. All we have to do is to ask and trust Him. When you feel sad, have heartache and sorrow, where else could you go? Who else could you turn to but Christ? Have you ever had a secret and told Jesus? Have you ever known Him to tell anyone? He is our friend and our parent(s) if we need one. Christ only asks us to trust Him, love Him and keep His commandments. And He asks us to love one another as He has loved us. He doesn't ask us to be pretty, have the finest clothes, the most money, the best talent in order to get into heaven. You can't fool Him nor can you bribe Him.

Now let's look at man's contests. We stand wanting man to notice us, love us, and make us great in their eyes. We will smile the best, wear the finest clothes, and tell man how much our clothes and shoes cost to impress them. When we hear them talking about all of our accomplishments, we think we have really made it in life. And when we show our talent we feel so proud and we think we accomplished this on our own. We forget where our gift comes from. We leave God out when we get the praise. Which contest do you want to win? Christ said, if you love me and keep my commandments and love one another, when I come again to take you to heaven I will have my rewards with me. And you will live forever with me and my Father in heaven (Rev. 22:12) and eat of the tree of life, with no more sickness, no death, no black, white, red, or yellow. Just all children of God. We will walk the streets of gold, sing with the angels, and live in the new Jerusalem. We will not need the material things of this old earth. We will just live and reign with Christ and His Father forevermore. Oh, by the grace of God will we want to be in this number.

Now, back to man's contest. You will have to look your best, have the most money, wear the latest fashions, live in the most fabulous home and try to impress someone in "high" places. All of this could help you win. But, if you are unfortunate not to be in the three finalists, well you haven't a chance to win. And all the work you have prepared and the long hours are in vain. Oh, what a loss. Now for the three finalists. **Winner number three** probably receives a small plaque with a small cash prize. Of course, there will be a clap from the crowd. That's all you get for all that preparation that you have done. Then there's **winner number two**. Well, when you hear that you were not number three for a short time you had a little hope that you might be the winner. But soon you find out that you are not. For your effort you receive a larger plaque and a larger cash prize. Maybe the claps were greater but do you have anything? After doing your very best, what do you have to show for it? Now, there's **winner number one**! Oh, how good you must feel! The crowd roars! The people even give you a standing ovation! For your prize you receive a very large plaque, a very large cash prize and even a car! You have it all! The whole world is at your fingertips. What a big prize! Everyone wants to be in your shoes for a while! You have all the attention from the world!

What happens when the contest is over and there is a new contest? And you lose and everyone forgets you. Where are all the friends, your money and your fame? It is all over. You have nothing, nothing at all. You see Christ coming in the clouds, and there you are standing with your plaque, your money, and the great talent that you used to please man, not God! IS IT WORTH IT? IS ANYTHING WORTH LOSING YOUR SOUL.

Is It Real Or Is It Memorex?

One day, about four years ago, I was on my way to work. I had to take a bus because my car was down. It was very early in the morning — about 6:00 a.m. I got off of the bus in front of Washington Park. To my amazement I saw people sleeping in the park. It was in the summer but, since it was so early, it was very cold that morning. After I arrived at work I couldn't quit talking about it. I was telling my friends that we should take the people in the park blankets and coats. They all agreed, but soon I started back driving and I quickly forgot about the people in the park. To my surprise some years later my sons, Lawrence and Robert, got together and brought some food and some small containers of juices and went to the park to feed the people. The next week the rest of us joined them in the park. It was such a great feeling doing something for someone else. So, from that time on, every Sabbath after church my family and I went to the park — winter or summer, rain or shine. We came together to feed God's people.

One day, as we were feeding the people, we met some people out of Milford who were also there to feed the people. So we formed a team that day and we planned meals for them. We prayed and we sang praises to God in the park. We did all that we could to help the ones who were less fortunate than we were. Week after week we met. Lawrence preached his first sermon there. He really let the Holy Spirit use him that day. That was the first time we knew that he could preach. Oh my God, how great is thy name. Week after week, we served the people. Larry preached the word to them. At first the people would get their food and just look at Larry as they went past him. Very few of them would stop and listen. Of course we had our share of hecklers. As time went by, the people started to respect him and they would stop and listen to the message that was delivered. Everything was going great. Members from our other group started to testify to how good God was. We formed a prayer circle and anyone who wanted special prayer would join our circle. Prayer after prayer went up to the Lord and we always gave all the praise to God.

I remembered our first Christmas together. God was so good to us. There was at least five churches joined together that day. The people had so much food to eat — including homemade rolls, roast, mixed vegetables, rice with gravy, and mashed potatoes. There were many cakes and cookies. They even had a tree, and we brought decorations for it. We let the children put the decorations on it. One church brought gifts for the people. They had hats and gloves for everyone. They even took the time to gift-wrap them all. The Lord really did bless that day. We worked together for many months until, one day, one of the members of the other group decided that he didn't want to come to the prayer line. That was very strange. The next time, we had a mixup in the food. Another time, we made 300 biscuits so they brought so many biscuits that we had to take ours back home.

Things like that started to creep up into our unity, our togetherness. Our love for one another seemed to begin to dissolve. We really didn't quite know what was wrong.

One day Larry received a phone call from the leader of the other group saying that they wouldn't be downtown for the next two weeks. That was the start of the breakup of our groups. Now we don't work together at all. But, looking back, when they would come downtown they would tell us how God had blesssed them with vans, money, freezers, and a pantry. They had a place to get vetgetables and meat at a discount. Now, all of a sudden, they no longer wanted to work with us. Why? I don't have any idea. I just know that we had a beautiful relationship and, one day, it was gone. Yes, we saw little warning signs. You see, Satan tries every way he can to break up a good thing. So he showed his ugly head in our program and caused us to separate. It reminds me of the Garden of Eden. Everything that God had made was perfect. But, instead of Eve focusing in on all of the beautiful things God had provided for her and her husband, she kept looking at this one tree. God told them not to go near it — not to touch it or eat the fruit of it — and that's how Satan got her. Satan could not go after them like he does us. Eve went to the tree and he started on her.

Let us look at our lives today. As long as we keep our eye on Christ and not ourselves, Satan cannot get control of our programs. Always remember, when God blesses us with material things in life, it is not that we are so good that we deserve it. God is just so merciful. He knows our needs before we ask Him for them. But it is what we do with the blessings that God gives to us that counts. Do we sit around and brag about all that we have accomplished, giving the credit to ourselves instead of God? Use the blessings that God gives to you to try to help the ones who are less fortunate. That way God will continue to bless and keep you. Then Satan can't come in and separate you from God. In Matt. 25:34-40, Jesus says, "I was hungry and you gave me meat, thirsty and you gave me drink". That's why our pots are cooked just right, because Jesus said inasmuch as you have done it unto one of the least of these my brethren ye have done it unto me.

So we cook for the homeless as if they were our special guests who we have invited to dinner. If we could see Jesus, if He came home with us for dinner, we would give Him our very best. That's the way we should treat His little ones — just like we had Jesus down in the park. We thank God that He permits us to help His children by feeding them and witnessing to them. So Lord keep us humble and faithful, and Jesus we pray that we keep our eyes on thee and thee only. In the name of Jesus, we pray.

P.S. JESUS, PLEASE MAKE OUR LOVE REAL — NOT MEMOREX!

Work While It is Day

Today is the day that the Lord has made, so we have to work while it is day. Tomorrow is not promised to us. Nightfall will be coming soon so today is the day you work in the fields for the Lord, seeking out the lost sheep. Our job is to gather in the sheep just like the shepherd in the field. He searches and searches until he has found all of his sheep. He won't go home nor will he stop until all of his sheep are found. That's the way we must learn to be. We must be willing to go all the way with Christ by our side. We have to be willing to become a servant, to serve others like Christ when He was in the Upper Room. He should have been waited on but instead He wrapped a towel around His waist and proceeded to wash His disciples' feet. How many of us would bend down to wash another's feet? I know that we wash feet at church. I mean someone who is homeless. Would you give them a bath, or how about changing some grown person's diaper? Or could you put your arms around a person who has a problem and give them the help that they need? How about money? Could you give a person your money to help them out without looking for your money back?

Have you ever taken the time to visit the elderly, to sit down and talk to them, maybe cook them a meal, take them for a ride, or go shopping for them? Or how about just listening to them as they tell you about their past. They just love for you to tell them about your children and grandchildren. Most of their families are gone now. They are all alone. But your talking to them brings back sweet memories of the past. We need to go to the highways and byways looking for all of God's lost souls. Some of God's precious souls don't even know that they are lost. They think that everything is just fine. Some of God's precious souls don't know anything about God's love.

That is our job to tell them about God's love and how much He loves them and He is always there just waiting for them to open their hearts and let Christ in. God loved us so much that He gave His only begotten Son to die for our sins.

There are too many people looking for love in all the wrong places. They are looking for love in drugs and so many other addictions. At first it feels like the real thing. They feel good but, after a short time, the good feeling goes away. So they try more and more drugs, different kinds — anything just trying to find that first good feeling that they once had. Then all of a sudden you can no longer hold on. It feels just like a dream when you dream you are falling, falling down, down, down — but you never hit the bottom. Being on drugs is not a dream. It is real, very much real. Once you put drugs in your body you know that it is not a dream. But it is reality. Once you start using drugs you just can't stop. You just keep on using and making excuses until, at the end, the drugs that you depended on — that you trusted with your life — will kill you.

God depends on His Shepherds to work in the fields to seek and find His lost sheep that need God's help. Sometimes just a friendly word, just a prayer or a hug will make all the difference. Remind them that God loves them and He will never leave them alone. Our young people are looking for love any way they can find it, so they join a gang. The members make-believe that they love this young person. They make-believe that they have a sweet and loving environment for them to belong to until they get them involved in all of the gang's activity. Then they turn on them. They show that young person all of their violence and all of their abuse. Sometimes the violence and abuse are used on the young person and sometimes it is used on others. The young person soon finds out that they are trapped. They can't get away. They feel that they have no future, so they are just waiting to die or to be put in jail. God's shepherds, where are you? Why can't we reach out and find these young people? Why can't we tell them that Christ loves them and there is no violence and there is no abuse in Christ — just love, pure love.

You just don't know what a person might be going through. The way you, as a Christian, approach that young person might be the difference between life and death in their lives. The way the Lord went from city to city healing the sick and feeding the people is the way we should work to save God's Lost Sheep. We love to dress up in our finest and have to get our cars shining so bright, but are we to dress up to tend to that person who might need a meal or a bath — or a child who might need its nose blown. Are our cars too shiny and new for us to pick up a person who is not as clean as we are, and are we willing to pack clothes or food for the homeless in our new car? If not, then we cannot be a shepherd for the Lord. God loves us all. Just because you didn't take the same path as that person who is on drugs or that young person who thought that if they would join a gang they will be loved, doesn't mean you are somehow "more" and they are "less". They might have to reach "rock bottom" before they can get the help that they need. You are not better than that person, you were just steered in another direction. You took another path and maybe God has made you a little stronger so that you can reach out and touch that person who is less fortunate than you are.

Once you have helped someone else, you know that you have seen the face of God. You have seen His face in that person who you have helped. They see God's face in you. The way you treat other people is the way others see God through you. You can't do God's work by sitting in church singing and praising the Lord in your own little space, thinking that you are okay with the Lord. Just because we get up and attend church every week, we think that someone else will do the job of helping others. That is not enough. We have to become a Shepherd for the Lord. We have to get out into the fields to work while it is day. Tonight is falling soon. Don't wait until tomorrow to reach out and touch that person

DO IT TODAY! RIGHT NOW! Who knows, you might not have another chance!

Grass Is Always Greener on the Other Side of the Street

We sit and look at the neighbors on the other side of the street. Sometimes we have to use binoculars so that we can see into their homes. Wow! They seem to have everything — a big beautiful home that must have cost them millions. They not only have an expensive car, but also have a van and a boat. The dog must have cost them a lot, too. Even the two children, a boy and a girl, attend the most expensive school. When they leave their house, everything seems perfect. The children appear to be well-behaved. The husband and wife seem to love each other. They walk right by us as though they didn't even see us — as they go to their jobs. One is a doctor, and the other a lawyer. We watch them as they come and go. As soon as they come home, we start watching to see what they are doing. We get all caught up with what is going on across the street so much until we forget all the wonderful things that God has done for us all of our lives. We sit and wish that we had the things that our neighbors own — instead of thanking God for all the things that we are blessed with.

Maybe you don't have that big house your neighbor has, but you have a home that you can afford. You have nice furniture and your house looks very nice. But, you can't see the things that you have because you are too busy looking at all the things that your neighbor has. Maybe you have more children than your neighbors have. You might feel that they are a burden. But you are blessed! You think that their two children are better than yours because they attend very important schools. Although your children attend public school, they can become the very best that they can because God has given you these children to raise and, by the grace of God, you have very beautiful children. They are not "caught up" in drugs. They are not in jail. They have nice jobs and are very respectful. What more do you want?

You spend so much time watching the neighbors coming and going that you forget all the blessings that you have. How do you know that their children are so wonderful and well-mannered? How do you know that couple is as loving behind closed doors as they are in public? And that big house with all the expensive furniture — how do you know they can pay for it? You need to stop being nosy where there is no concern of yours. You need to stop dreaming about what's going on on the other side of the street and think about how good God has been to you and your family.

We buy magazines and just go crazy when we read about how the movie stars live. We spend so much time dreaming about other people's good fortune and wishing that is was us. Count your blessings! Have you ever had a day without food to eat? Did you ever have a sickness and was all alone with no one to help you? Do you have money to buy food and pay rent? Did you buy clothes and shoes? Can you and your family go on vacations? Do you drive a nice car?

How many televisions and v.c.r.'s do you have in your home? And these are just a few things we have in our houses. Are we thankful for what we have? I don't think so because, if we were, we would not be jealous of our neighbor. Instead we would say, "My neighbor has a lot of material things that are here today and gone tomorrow". The things that we should be collecting are Heavenly things that not only are here today but will be here tomorrow.

You just know how blessed you are when all of your children are still here and they are healthy. When you look at all the children who are sick and their parents don't know if they will be around for tomorrow, who cares if they go to expensive schools or if they wear expensive clothes? The only thing those parents want is for their child to be healthy. They will give all the money in the world just to have a child who can get up and run around like other children. From now on when you see someone with more than you have, stop dreaming about all the riches that they have and count your blessings. Start counting them from the time you were a child to now. Do you think that you can count them? Do you think you even remember them? But the Lord still takes care of us. He takes care of us from our birth until our death. How lucky we are to have such a wonderful Savior. Because we have such a Savior, we don't have to worry about the neighbor on the other side of the street.

Much Prayer, Much Power; Little Prayer, Little Power

The link between God and man is prayer. Let's look at the power of prayer. If Adam and Eve had kept on praying and kept their eyes on God, they would never have failed. Satan could never have come between Adam and Eve and God (Gen. 3:1-24). And if Cain had looked to God and followed His instructions, he would never have allowed his jealousy to come between his brother, Abel, and himself. Noah was a praying man and God saved Noah and his whole family. Abraham was a man of God and God took care of him (Gen. 4:3-15, Gen. 6 and 7). Moses found out about the love of God and he learned to totally trust in God (Gen. 24). Through prayer he led the children through the wilderness. Elijah believed in God and did just what God told him to do and God took him to heaven without dying (2 Kings). Elisha, who took Elijah's place, also trusted God and God worked miracle after miracle in his life until his dying day. Elisha prayed and trusted in the Lord. Men like Job, David, and Joseph prayed and trusted in God. Daniel, who ended up in a foreign land prayed three times a day. He never did forget the Lord and the Lord never forgot him. Because of his faithfulness, God saved him from the lions' den (Dan. 6). And Daniel's three friends Shadrach, Meshach and Abednago were delivered by God for their faithfulness from the fiery furnace (Dan. 3). If you are faithful to God, He will see you through.

Then look at the life of Jesus himself while on this earth. He kept in touch with His father the whole time He was here. In Gethsmane, Jesus prayed not as "I will", but "thy will be done". That's the way we should pray to our Father in heaven (Matt. 26-39). When the disciples finally learned to trust in Jesus, oh what a difference it made in their lives. We need to learn to trust in the Father. We need to learn to talk to the Father as a friend. Sometimes we say our prayers and our blessings as a rhyme. As a child you learned, "Now I lay me down to sleep I pray the Lord my soul to keep". But God is our Father and friend. Do we talk to our friends in rhyme? Or do we talk to our friends about anything that comes into mind? That's the way we should talk to our heavenly Father — our friend. Tell Him what is on your mind, what you need, and don't forget to ask for others and their needs (Therefore I say unto you what things so ever ye desire when ye pray, believe that ye receive them and ye shall have them — Mark 11:24).

Prayer is the key in the hands of faith to unlock heaven's storehouse (as I Jesus say unto you ask and it shall be given you, seek and ye shall find, knock and it shall be opened unto you. For everyone that asketh receiveth and to him that knocketh it shall be opened — Luke 11:9-10). What is prayer? Prayer is the opening of the heart to God as to a friend. Prayer is communion with heaven — a two-way conversation between God and man. Come to Jesus just as you are. If sin has broken the connection between you and God, come in prayer and complete the circuit again (I say unto you that likewise joy shall be in heaven over one sinner that repenteth, more than over ninty and nine just persons which need no repentance — Luke 15:7).

When we pray we may wish to follow the outline of the prayer given by Jesus in the Sermon on the Mount found in Matt. 6:9-13, "Our Father which are in Heaven..." This is the pattern Jesus gave. We are to come to God as His children addressing him as our Father and reverently giving Him honor. We are to pray for His will to be done in our hearts on this earth as it is in heaven. Scripture says, "Give us this day our daily bread". We are to recognize that every good gift comes from God. We should never forget to thank Him for these blessings. And this prayer further states, "And forgive us our debts as we forgive our debtors. And lead us not into temptation, but deliver us from evil; for thine is the Kingdom, and the power, and the glory, for ever, and ever — Amen". We are to ask forgiveness of our sins. We are to recognize that our ability to resist sin comes from God. Our Father is made glad when we are truly happy. His heart warms when our heart goes out to Him — expressing our love for Him Jesus taught us to make our requests to the Father in His name. There are many things in our lives and on our hearts that we do not feel free to discuss with even our most intimate friends. With Jesus it is different. We can and should open our hearts to Him intimately and in private. He knows and understands our innermost feelings, joys, and our love for Him. Our heart's longings, our weaknesses and our sins all are open to His understanding. For we have not a high priest which cannot be touched with the feelings or our infirmaties. But was in all points tempted, like as we are, yet without sin. Let us therefore come boldly unto the throne of grace that we may obtain mercy and find grace to help in time of need (Heb. 4:15-16). Are you afraid? Are you worried? Then pray. Every personal problem that burdens your heart may be taken to God in private prayer. Prayer brings us within the circle of His mercy where His grace is ours to the full extent of our need.

The A B C D's of Prayer:

A Ask and it shall be given you (Matt. 7:7). Ask anything in my name — J.E.S.U.S. I will do it. The Father may be glorified in the Son (John 14:13-14).

B Believe ye that I am able to do this? They say unto Him ye Lord (Matt. 9:28). But without faith it is impossible to please Him.

C Call upon me in the day of trouble and I will deliver thee and thou shall glorify me (Ps. 50).

D Delight thyself also in the Lord and He shall give thee the desire of thine heart (Ps. 37:4).

We Are All God's Children

Life is such a wonderful miracle! Consider how a baby is conceived inside of its mother's womb. And how it grows larger and larger until it is time for its birth. It seems so complicated but, yet, it is the most fascinating thing to watch. And when that little person comes down the birth canal and you see the top of its little head peep out, everyone is excited. No one stops the baby being born or says, "Oh, no — it's not the right race. Put it back!" No! Regardless of the color of the baby's skin when its little head appears and its little body shoots out we feel, "What a beautiful miracle we have just witnessed". At that moment no one is caring about race or prejudices. And, in the nursery, the babies are all alike. The only thing different is the color of their skin. They are just darling little babies just coming into the world. When the babies cry, they all sound alike. You cannot tell the color of the baby's skin by the sound of his voice. They are treated alike.

Children are not born knowing how to hate. They have to be taught how to hate and discriminate. Generation after generation of people live their lives, make their accomplishments and their failures, and the children are taught their prejudices and hate. They instill in their children's' lives their values whether they are right or wrong. They live their lives and then move on and a new generation takes over. Generation after generation the prejudices and hate go on. Some races feel that they are inferior to other races. Others feel they are better and no other race is as good as theirs. But we all are made in the image of God.

At one time, all people were the same. After the flood there was Noah, his wife, his sons — Shem, Ham and Japher — and their wives. They repopulated the earth. At this time, everyone spoke the same language until the people decided to build a tower to reach all the way to Heaven so that they would never be destroyed by water again. God came down and saw what was going on. He found them working hard at building their tower so He changed their language so that they could no longer understand each other. So when one would ask for brick, others gave them something else because they did not understand what was being asked of them. The ones who spoke the same language went off together to different parts of the earth. That's how we became different colors. The ones who moved closer to the sun, the darker their skin became. And the farther away from the sun, the lighter the skin. But that doesn't make us different. The only thing different is the color of our skin.

We all hurt alike! We bleed alike! We love alike! We all live our lives and, when it is over, we die! Regardless of the color of our skin, we are all alike! At one time, were we not the descendants of Noah's three son's? Didn't we work together and speak the same languages? At one time we were all one family. What could ever make a race of people think they are better than other people just because of their color, their education, their poverty? How dare we treat one another the way that we do? When Jesus looks down and sees the way we treat the ones who he and His Father made in their own image, it hurts Him. And we act as though they don't even exist just because they are different than we are! Jesus will show all of us just how He feels about prejudice and hate!

When we are with Jesus, there will not be any separation there. So if we can't live together now, how will we live together in Heaven? One day Jesus will put His arms around the ones who other races have hated and mistreated from generation to generation and shower all of His love upon them and show them that they are EVERYTHING TO HIM. Jesus loves us all. He did not die for just a few. HE DIED FOR US ALL — regardless of race! When Jesus looks upon us, He is not judging based on the color of our skin. Have you ever seen a rainbow after it has rained? There are such wonderful colors. It looks as though God Himself has taken the time to paint it just right. That's the way God's people are — a perfect rainbow all of different colors.

Just imagine if every person from every race would open their hearts and stretch their arms from city to city and state to state and country to country and clasp the hand of their brothers and sisters with love as Christ has commanded us to do,

WHAT A BEAUTIFUL SIGHT THAT WOULD BE!

Faith

Without faith, it is impossible to please Him. *For he that cometh to God must believe that He is a rewarder of them that diligently seek Him* (Heb. 11:6). That's the whole point! We have to believe that Jesus can make a big difference in our lives. Faith is about belief. We should learn to put our WHOLE trust in the Lord through His word, through much prayer and even through nature. We will get to know Him and trust Him. A lot of times we have hopes and dreams. We would love to have our whole life planned out and, if it falls through, we blame God. Let's just see if it's God's fault. First of all, did you talk to God about your plans? Did you wait for an answer? Or did you bullheadily jump off of your knees and start putting your plans in motion? And, when it fails, we want to blame God. When you read about God's love or just look around at all the things in the world that you just can't really explain where they come from, like how a baby is born, this will deepen your faith. There are so many miracles in the world that no one can explain.

When you believe in the Lord Jesus Christ, you know there is a God. You can tell a person about the love of God. You can talk for many hours telling them to have faith in Jesus. But, until this person gets to know Jesus for themselves and until they let Jesus into his or her life, they will not experience that inner peace that Jesus brings. Then, he will have all of the faith in our Savior that he needs. The Disciples, when they walked with Jesus, saw Him do miracle after miracle. They saw all of the works that Jesus did. They even helped Him. They were impressed, but the Disciples had more on their minds than miracles. It was not until after His death and resurrection and the Holy Spirit came in that they truly understood what Jesus was trying to teach them. Sometimes, we are so busy that we can't listen to what Jesus is trying to teach us. HAVE FAITH IN GOD! Faith is a word that we learn about through experience from all that God has brought us through.

Now faith is the substance of things hoped for the evidence of things not seen (Heb. 11:6). Let's look to God in faith believing that *I can do all things through Christ which strengthen me (Phil 4:13).* And Jesus answered and said unto them:

HAVE FAITH IN GOD FOR VERILY I SAY UNTO YOU,
THAT WHOSOEVER SHALL SAY UNTO THIS MOUNTAIN
BE THOU REMOVED AND BE THE CAST INTO THE SEA
AND SHALL NOT DOUBT IN HIS HEART
BUT SHALL BELIEVE THAT THOSE THINGS WHICH HE SAID
SHALL COME TO PASS
HE SHALL HAVE WHATSOEVER HE SAID (Mark 11:22).

Special Holidays

There are two very special holidays that we Americans keep that seem to change our lives completely. We become so loving and kind at this time of year. Now there are 365 days in a year, including these two special holidays, which are Thanksgiving and Christmas. On our daily routine, you might pass by a homeless person every day. Maybe you have to go around them because you are late and they are in your way. And you might wonder why they are not working or at least looking for a job. And what about that elderly person who you know about who might need a helping hand with groceries, cleaning, or even maybe cooking a meal? You always meant to stop in and help but you just don't have the time. Then there is the person that just needs someone to reach out and offer them your love and support. But we don't have the time to stop to help. We are too busy trying to make that almighty dollar.

Now, for 363 days, it seems as though we have no feelings or no heart. But Thanksgiving is the first of the special holidays. It seems as though our hearts start to melt and we start to feel sorry for others as we plan for this big meal that we cook for Thanksgiving. We start to wonder if that elderly person has somewhere to go for Thanksgiving and, if they are unable to come out, you plan to carry their dinner to them so that they will have a wonderful Thanksgiving dinner. You even call all around town trying to find out who is cooking for the homeless. Now you want to help. You are even willing to cook and even serve them. On Thanksgiving day you serve hundreds of homeless people, elderly people, even drug addicts, and lonely people. These people just don't have anyplace to go or seem so all alone. But, this day, you are willing to step in to make this day wonderful for them because they are the less fortunate. And, of course, the evening news will carry the story of how these good people took time out of their busy day to make sure these poor people had a beautiful Thanksgiving dinner.

Now you feel pretty good about yourself. You have done your Christian duty for another year. You are all warmed up now. Thanksgiving has passed and you go back to your regular routine. But Christmas is coming and you start thinking about your children and the rest of your family. You know that you are well blessed and you start to feel guilty because you know that you have so much, and you are aware of families that don't have half of the things that yours has. So when you see different groups asking for money to help the less fortunate you are willing to give a few dollars. And, as Christmas arrives, we don't mind adding another Christmas gift for a needy person. You even deliver the gifts and cook and serve the needy again. Just like Thanksgiving you want the homeless, the elderly, the drug addict and anyone who doesn't have a Christmas dinner to have the best Christmas dinner that they ever had.

You feel so good about yourself because you feel that you have done a good deed. You have — and that's good that you feel good about yourself and, when you are sitting around the house with your family, you want them to know what you did. You want them to know how much you love the needy. Your family helps out. They see just how generous you are. But the day after Thanksgiving and the day after Christmas, these same people wake up to the same conditions that they had at Thanksgiving and Christmas. They are either homeless, elderly, and still on drugs or they still need someone to love them. When we go back to our routine in life, after the holidays, don't act like these people don't exist. They need help the other 363 days in the year. Let's learn to always try to help others.

This is the lesson that we want to share with our families. Just like you feel so good about yourself on these special holidays, you will feel good about yourself each and every day. Let's have a little compassion for one another. Remember it could have been you homeless, on drugs, elderly, sick or lonely. God doesn't only bless you two days out of a year. HE BLESSES YOU EACH AND EVERY DAY. Let your children see you loving and caring for your brothers and sisters EACH AND EVERY DAY — not only on Thanksgiving and Christmas.

The End of the Year

Well, it's here again — another December 31 — the end of the year as it is called, New Year's Eve. All around the country huge parties are being planned. The television advertisements were busy with information about parties that will be going on starting December 31. People run around shopping for that special outfit and buying all kinds of party supplies — spending up so much money just to celebrate the new year. What are we celebrating? A year of ups and downs? A year of rushing around working long hours at a job just to pay bills from one month to another? Dealing with our children? Sometimes they are so out of control, it seems that they don't care about anything or anyone — with all of the killing, stealing and raping going on. Drugs and guns are everywhere. It used to be that crime happened only in poor neighborhoods. But now drugs, guns and killing, as well as child abusing and stealing, are everywhere — in everyone's neighborhood. So what are we celebrating? Are we hoping that the new year coming in will be different? Do we think that our problems will go away in the new year because, now, things are so bad that we can't ignore them anymore?

There used to be a time that when our children went to school, they were safe. But now, when they leave the house, you're in fear for their lives at school because children bring guns and knives to school and will use them without thinking about it. Then there are the drug dealers who don't care about ruining a young child's mind for that almighty dollar. How could we find pleasure in knowing that a new year is coming in and we have no idea what the future holds for each of us? No one knows what the future will be! No one but God Almighty. In our daily lives we act as though the clock has control or do we? We are always in a hurry. We never have time to take a break — to slow down, to be with our families.

The first thing parents want to do is give the children money to do whatever they want to do, or tell them to look at television. Anything to keep them amused on their own, to prepare their own meals, or to take care of younger brothers and sisters while the parents are rushing from place to place trying to make money for that home or new car. But the only thing is they never get enough. They always have to have more. So the harder they work, the more the clock moves on. We are now watching the hands of the clock as it slowly moves up towards 12:00. We are waiting for the new year to come in. We have already started making our new year's resolutions — making all kinds of promises for the new year — knowing that we will never keep them. But year after year, we make them faithfully.

As we wait for the hands of the clock to reach 12, we think about our lives and all of the things that have happened to us this whole year. We can't change the decisions that we made this year because, in a very few minutes, this year will be over. But there is another year about to come in. Did we learn anything from our mistakes? Or will we take the same problems into the new year that we had in the year that passed? With all of the terrible things that are going on everyday all around us, you can't turn on the news without nearly busting out into tears because of all of the violence that we see going on all around us. As we watch the hands of the clock, it climbs closer and closer towards 12:00. We listen patiently as the clock ticks, ticks, ticks away. With our drinks in hand, we become so excited about the coming of the new year. As we laugh, talk and drink we wonder why we're so happy? Just what do we have to celebrate? We become very quiet. We sit our glasses down. We no longer watch the clock because our minds are thinking about our lives this past year. And the things that have happened to us and all of our family members this year. We wonder about the future. How many of us will be alive to see the end of this new year.

Instead of us watching the clock for the start of the new year, we decide to CALL ON JESUS. We start to testify and sing the praises to our God. We pray that the Lord will be a part of our lives in the new year. As we hold hands and sing the praises of the Lord, we find out what we need in our lives for the new year is JESUS — AND THEN THE CLOCK STRUCK 12 AND THE NEW YEAR BEGINS.

About the Author

After finishing this book I decided to use my first name and middle initial. So the name on my book is LORETTA V. I decided not to use a last name. I didn't have a good marriage but I was Blessed with six children. All of my children are now grown and they have children of their own. I am now Blessed with twenty-one grandchildren and seven great grandchildren. One day I became very ill and I was admitted into the hospital. I was diagnose with a disease that I had never heard of before. After a week I was released and sent home. After I arrived home I lived alone and I was up all night, I couldn't sleep at night. And the Lord used that time to speak to me and I started to write down the message the Lord had given me. Sometimes the Lord has work for us to do and we have to listen for that still small voice. And I have been doing the Lord's work ever since.

www.ingramcontent.com/pod-product-compliance
Lightning Source LLC
Chambersburg PA
CBHW022219050726
47590CB00002B/867